The Nature of
Conspiracy Theories

The Nature of Conspiracy Theories

Michael Butter

Translated by Sharon Howe

polity

Originally published in German as '*Nichts ist, wie es scheint*': *Über Verschwörungstheorien* © Suhrkamp Verlag Berlin 2018. All rights reserved by and controlled through Suhrkamp Verlag Berlin

This English edition © 2020 by Polity Press

Polity Press
65 Bridge Street
Cambridge CB2 1UR, UK

Polity Press
101 Station Landing
Suite 300
Medford, MA 02155, USA

ISBN-13: 978-1-5095-4081-5
ISBN-13: 978-1-5095-4082-2 (paperback)

A catalogue record for this book is available from the British Library.

Library of Congress Cataloging-in-Publication Data

Names: Butter, Michael, author.
Title: The nature of conspiracy theories / Michael Butter ; translated by
    Sharon Howe.
Other titles: "Nichts ist, wie es scheint". English
Description: Cambridge, UK ; Medford, MA : Polity Press, 2020. | Includes
    bibliographical references and index. | Summary: "A comprehensive
    introduction to conspiracy theories and their growing presence in the
    age of the internet"-- Provided by publisher.
Identifiers: LCCN 2020008369 (print) | LCCN 2020008370 (ebook) | ISBN
    9781509540815 (hardback) | ISBN 9781509540822 (paperback) | ISBN
    9781509540839 (epub)
Subjects: LCSH: Conspiracy theories. | History--Errors, inventions, etc.
Classification: LCC HV6275 .B8813 2020 (print) | LCC HV6275 (ebook) |
    DDC 001.9--dc23
LC record available at https://lccn.loc.gov/2020008369
LC ebook record available at https://lccn.loc.gov/2020008370

Typeset in 10.5 on 12pt Sabon
by Fakenham Prepress Solutions, Fakenham, Norfolk NR21 8NL
Printed and bound in Great Britain by TJ International Limited

For further information on Polity, visit our website: politybooks.com

Contents

Acknowledgements

It is a great pleasure to thank the many people who 'conspired' with me on this project in manifold ways over the past years. Daniel Graf planted the idea for this book in my mind many years ago and finally made me pursue it. Elise Heslinga and John Thompson at Polity were a pleasure to work with. So were Heinrich Geiselberger and Nora Mercurio at Suhrkamp, which published the original German version in 2018. Special thanks are due to Sharon Howe for not getting lost in my overly long German sentences while translating the book. That I felt that I had something to say at all is mostly due to the impact of a number of wonderful colleagues who shared their ideas with me over the years. I am thinking in particular of the members of the COST Action 'Comparative Analysis of Conspiracy Theories', many of whom have become good friends over the past years. I am especially indebted to Peter Knight, Andrew McKenzie-McHarg and Claus Oberhauser. I would also like to acknowledge the impact that Andreas Anton has had on my thoughts about conspiracy theories. I mention him only in one endnote (and completely forgot to mention him in the German edition), but his take on conspiracy theories as a form of knowledge had a lasting effect on me. Finally, I would like to thank my research assistants Alexandra Dempe and Hannah Herrera for tracking down references, formatting endnotes and bearing with me when I decided to change something once again.

Introduction, or: What's the plan?

On 8 February 1920, the *Illustrated Sunday Herald* published a short speech by Winston Churchill with the title 'Zionism versus Bolshevism: A Struggle for the Soul of the Jewish People'. In this speech, delivered to Churchill's old regiment at Aldershot a few days earlier, the future British prime minister reflects on the role of the Jews in the Russian communist revolution of 1917, and the ongoing civil war it has sparked. Drawing on a plethora of anti-Semitic stereotypes, Churchill distinguishes between three types of Jews, 'two of which', he suggests, 'are helpful and hopeful in a very high degree to humanity, and the third absolutely destructive'. The two groups of Jews that Churchill views positively – '"National" Jews' and Zionists – have in common that they subscribe to the spirit of nationalism so prevalent in Europe at the time, and not only among conservatives. The ones he eyes suspiciously are the 'International Jews' who he aligns with the menace of communism.[1]

Churchill expresses respect for those Jews who, 'dwelling in every country throughout the world, identify themselves with that country, enter into its national life, and, while adhering faithfully to their own religion, regard themselves as citizens in the fullest sense of the State which has received them'. Still, as the final words of this sentence – resonating with the idea of the Jews as homeless and wandering – make clear, Churchill cannot quite shed the idea that the Jews do not properly belong to the national body politic. In his view, they are guests in the nations that have offered them a place to live and should behave accordingly. He also has only praise for the attempts to create 'by the banks of the Jordan a Jewish State under the protection of the British Crown', a project he presents as both significantly driven by British Jews and 'in harmony with the truest interests of the British Empire'.

By contrast, he views the alleged activities of the third group – the 'International Jews' – as highly problematic and a threat to the stability of the global order in general and to Britain and its political system in particular. 'Most, if not all' of these Jews, he writes, 'have forsaken the faith of their forefathers, and divorced from their minds all spiritual hopes of the next world'. In their minds, religion has been replaced with ideology. Having turned communist, they now want to abolish not only religion but also the nation state. Their goal, according to Churchill, is to establish 'a world-wide communistic State'.

Somewhat surprisingly at first sight, Churchill claims that this idea is much older than communism itself, and it is here that his text becomes truly relevant for a book on conspiracy theories:

> This movement among the Jews is not new. From the days of Spartacus-Weishaupt to those of Karl Marx, and down to Trotsky (Russia), Bela Kun (Hungary), Rosa Luxembourg [sic] (Germany), and Emma Goldman (United States), this world-wide conspiracy for the overthrow of civilisation and for the reconstitution of society on the basis of arrested development, of envious malevolence, and impossible equality, has been steadily growing. It played, as a modern writer, Mrs. Webster, has so ably shown, a definitely recognisable part in the tragedy of the French Revolution. It has been the mainspring of every subversive movement during the Nineteenth Century; and now at last this band of extraordinary personalities from the underworld of the great cities of Europe and America have gripped the Russian people by the hair of their heads and have become practically the undisputed masters of that enormous empire.

According to Churchill, then, the rise of communism in Russia is the latest chapter in a 'world-wide conspiracy', led by 'extraordinary personalities', that has been going on since the eighteenth century.

It is therefore hardly surprising that scholars have not only labelled Churchill's speech anti-Semitic but also classified it as a conspiracy theory.[2] Conspiracy theories have become a focus of public attention over the last two decades, and it is no longer just academics who are quick to discover them in the past and the present. Long ignored by the public, conspiracy theories have now been omnipresent for some time. The suspicions regarding Jews, Freemasons and the Illuminati perpetuated in Churchill's speech remain all-pervasive. And they have been compounded ever since by a host of new allegations expanding on the older conspiracy theories, or in many cases even merging with them: that the USA carried out the 9/11 attacks itself; that we are being secretly controlled by a New World Order that keeps us docile via chemtrails; that the Ukrainian crisis was orchestrated by NATO; that Barack Obama was not born in the USA or that – along with Angela Merkel and George W. Bush – he belongs to an elite of extra-terrestrial reptilians that feeds upon our negative energy. Not to mention that the moon landing never happened, and that John F. Kennedy was murdered by the CIA.

Most recently, the COVID-19 pandemic has led to the emergence of a plethora of highly publicized conspiracist allegations. Some versions claim that the virus is either a Chinese or an American biological weapon which was, depending on the individual story, intentionally or accidentally released. Other versions hold that the virus does not exist or is completely harmless, and that dark forces – the 'deep state', Bill Gates, the World Health Organization, the New World Order or others – are using the hysteria to hurt Donald Trump, reduce the world population, or achieve other malicious goals. For the most part, these coronavirus conspiracy theories are adaptations of much older conspiracy narratives. Quite frequently, the current crisis is imagined to be merely the latest chapter in an ongoing plot and is thus simply grafted onto long-existing narrative templates. At any rate, the popularity of these conspiracy theories shows that revelations concerning alleged plots by countries, intelligence services, international institutions or groups of powerful individuals are no longer confined to subcultures, but are now reaching a wider public.[3]

Accordingly, many observers have concluded that conspiracy theories are more socially acceptable today than ever before, and that there has been a surge in the number of people believing in them. This has in turn alarmed those who remain sceptical – still the greater part of the population and the overwhelming majority of the media. Hence, the term 'conspiracy theory' has become a permanent fixture of everyday social discourse: barely a week goes by without it appearing in the evening news or the daily papers. Why a particular idea should be called a 'conspiracy theory' is never explained, however: apparently, this is something we all understand intuitively. 'I know it when I see it', an American judge once said about pornography, and the same applies to most of us when it comes to conspiracy theories. The present example is relatively clear-cut, and unless you subscribe to the myth of an international Jewish conspiracy and therefore believe Churchill to be simply stating a fact, you would probably describe his remarks as a conspiracy theory.

But what is it exactly about Churchill's speech that earns it this label? What distinguishes his form of conspiracy theorizing from that of Nesta Webster, the source he draws on? And how does the open articulation of an anti-Semitic conspiracy theory by perhaps the most important British politician of the twentieth century relate to the claim that conspiracy theories have recently been growing in popularity and influence? What role does the internet play in the spread of conspiracy theories, and how does it influence our belief in them? How long have conspiracy theories in general been around? What is the connection between conspiracy theories and populism? Who actually believes in them and why? Are they dangerous? And if so, what can we do about them?

The answers to these questions are much harder to find than conspiracy theories themselves. There is a glaring disparity between the heat with which the topic is currently discussed and the knowledge informing the vast majority of such discussions. All too often, ideas are described as conspiracy theories when they are not. Opponents of vaccination may be misguided, but not all of them are conspiracy theorists. Time and time again, different types of conspiracy theories are lumped together, whether they are directed against elites or minorities, and whether they are racist or not. And it is often assumed that that all conspiracy theories encourage violence, when their link with violence is in fact far more complex, as we shall see in the conclusion to this book.

Because of the upsurge of populism in Europe and the USA, and now the COVID-19 crisis, the concern about conspiracy theories has grown exponentially in recent years. In particular, the Brexit campaign and the election of Donald Trump as US president have rendered the public debate over conspiracy theories even more heated and unfocused, resulting for example in a blurring of boundaries between conspiracy theories and fake news. The coronavirus pandemic has done nothing to alleviate this conceptual confusion. But conspiracy theories and fake news are not the same. Conspiracy theories can be fake news – that is, false information deliberately circulated in order to discredit certain individuals and/or achieve some other objective. But not all conspiracy theories are fake news, and vice versa. Many conspiracy theorists are genuinely convinced that they have uncovered a plot; equally, not all deliberately circulated misinformation pertains to an alleged conspiracy. There is an important difference between claiming that concern about COVID-19 is exaggerated and contending that the panic is intentionally manufactured by dark forces in pursuit of some sinister goal.

The imprecise use of the term is not the only problem, however. Those who engage with conspiracy theories – and that goes for academics and journalists alike – often lack an adequate understanding of how they arise, what they do for those who believe in them, and what their potential consequences may be. This is due not least to the fact that only one study on the subject has so far had any notable and lasting impact on public perception: Richard Hofstadter's famous 1964 essay on the 'paranoid style in American politics'.[4] Even in the USA, where some dozen compelling books on the subject have been published since the 1990s, few in the media have yet come up with a response to Donald Trump's daily flirtation with conspiracism that doesn't refer to Hofstadter's essay.

Hofstadter, one of the most respected historians of his time, saw belief in conspiracy theories as bordering on clinical paranoia. By the same token, he claimed that, in the USA, the tendency to see conspiracies everywhere had always been confined to a minority on the margins of society. During the 2016 presidential campaign, the *New York Times*, the *Washington Post*, Salon.com, the *New Republic* and many other media outlets used Hofstadter's terminology to characterize

Trump, and to some extent they still do. Even Hillary Clinton made reference to Hofstadter on one of the rare occasions when she commented directly on Trump's conspiracy theories. At a hustings in Reno, Nevada in August 2016, she accused Trump of exploiting prejudices and paranoia, and appealed to moderate Republicans to resist the takeover of their party by the radical fringe.[5] Outside the USA, too, Hofstadter's text is still the most influential analysis of conspiracy theories to date. German media such as *Die Zeit* or *Die Welt* for example have also drawn on it in an attempt to understand the Trump phenomenon. Nor are things any better when it comes to other conspiracy theories: writing in August 2018, for instance, *Guardian* columnist Marina Hyde accused the followers of Jeremy Corbyn of 'do[ing] politics in the paranoid style'.[6]

Scholars who study conspiracy theories, however, have long since come to regard Hofstadter's text as outdated. While he makes many valid points, his pathologization of conspiracy theorists as paranoid is highly problematic. Moreover, given that – according to the latest empirical studies – half of the population of the USA, and nearly as many in most European countries, believe in at least one conspiracy theory, it is also completely meaningless.[7] Other aspects of Hofstadter's argument have proved wrong, too. In short, when it comes to understanding what conspiracy theories are and how they work, neither our intuition nor the one study which has shaped the public understanding of the subject are of any help.

It is the purpose of this book to provide a more accurate account of conspiracy theories. By examining the underlying principles, functions, effects and history of conspiracist thinking, I hope to contribute to a better understanding of the phenomenon. Naturally, I focus on current developments, in particular the association of conspiracy theories with populist rhetoric, as well as the role of the internet in their dissemination. In order to make sense of the present, however, we need a historical perspective. After all, the history of conspiracy theories is also inevitably that of the changing public spheres in which they circulate, and of the media environments that shape them. If we want to understand how the internet – where counterpublics are formed so much more easily than outside the virtual environment, and where conspiracy theories can be continuously updated

– influences the forms and functions of conspiracist suspicions, we need to know what things were like before: that is, what influence other media regimes exerted in earlier times.

The crux of my argument is that it is, above all, the status of conspiracy theories in public discourse that has changed most radically over time, and that it is now changing once again. Even if it might feel like it at times, we are not living in a golden age of conspiracy theories. It is not true that conspiracism is more popular and influential now than ever before. On the contrary: conspiracy theories are currently generating so much discussion precisely because they are still a stigmatized form of knowledge whose premises are regarded with extreme scepticism by many people. And therein lies the difference between past and present. Up to the 1950s, the Western world regarded conspiracy theories as a perfectly legitimate form of knowledge whose underlying assumptions were beyond question. It was therefore normal to believe in them. Only after the Second World War did conspiracy theories begin to undergo a complex process of delegitimization in the USA and Europe, causing conspiracist knowledge to be banished from public discourse and relegated to the realm of subcultures.

On the one hand, the current 'renaissance' of conspiracy theories is partly connected with the rise of populist movements, in that there are structural parallels between populist and conspiracist arguments. On the other hand, the internet plays a key role because it has made conspiracy theories – which had flown under most people's radar for a while – highly visible and easily available again. In addition, the internet has been a catalyst for the fragmentation of the public sphere. What we are experiencing now is a situation where conspiracy theories are still stigmatized in some domains – particularly those we continue to regard as mainstream – but are being accepted once again as legitimate knowledge in others. It is the clash between these domains and their different conceptions of truth that is fuelling the current debate over such theories. While some people are fearful (once again) of conspiracies, others are (or remain) more concerned with the dire consequences of conspiracy theories. In this respect, you could say we are entering a third phase in the history of conspiracism. After the long period of widespread acceptance and the short one of complete stigmatization, we in the West are now living

in a world where conspiracy theories are simultaneously legitimate and illegitimate knowledge. Everything that is currently
discussed regarding these theories – who believes in them and
why and to what effects – needs to be understood against this
background.

In what follows, I develop this argument in six chapters,
arranged in such a way that they can also be read in isolation or
in a different order. In Chapter 1, I discuss various definitions
and typologies of conspiracy theories, noting in particular that
the term is not merely a neutral description but always implies
– at least in everyday discourse – a value judgement. Chapter
2 deals with the evidence used in conspiracy theories. What
arguments are put forward by believers, and how do they
tell the story of the plots they believe they have discovered?
In Chapter 3, I analyse the different functions of conspiracy
theories for individuals and groups, and discuss the question
of whether some people are more receptive to such theories
than others. Chapter 4 traces the historical development of
conspiracy theories from antiquity to the present, and ends
with a discussion of the relationship between conspiracy
theories and populism. Chapter 5 is devoted to the impact
of the internet on the visibility and status, as well as the
rhetoric and argumentation, of conspiracy theories. Using the
coronavirus crisis as a point of departure, the book concludes
by examining whether and in what circumstances conspiracy
theories are dangerous, and tackles the current controversy
over what to do about them.

As a German Americanist, I draw most of my examples
from the USA, the UK and the German-speaking countries,
but my analysis is not limited to these cultures. Due to my
systematic approach, my observations also apply to conspiracy
theories and cultures that I do not mention at all. However, my
perspective on conspiracy theories is that of a scholar trained
in literary and cultural studies. Much of what follows is the
consensus view across academic disciplines; on some issues,
though, opinions are divided, and a quantitative psychologist
would come to very different conclusions. I also raise questions
at various points which no discipline is currently able to answer
due to the fact that little or no research has been done in these
areas. In this respect, my book merely marks, if anything,
the end of the beginning of the study of conspiracy theories.
What goes for conspiracy theorists goes for conspiracy theory
researchers too: there is always more to learn.

1

'Everything is planned', or: What is a conspiracy theory?

Conspiracy theories assert the existence of a covertly operating group of people – the conspirators – who seek, from base motives and by underhand means, to achieve a certain end. The word 'conspiracy' comes from the Latin verb *conspirare*, meaning to be in harmony or act in concert. A conspiracy, whether real or imagined, is therefore never the work of one individual, but always of a group, whether large or small. But conspiracy theories have other typical characteristics, too, which I discuss in the first part of this chapter, once again using the example of Winston Churchill's text 'Zionism versus Bolshevism'. I then go on to consider some typologies that have been proposed for the classification of conspiracy theories. In particular, I distinguish between top-down, bottom-up, internal and external varieties, as well as between scenarios centring on a specific event, a specific group of conspirators or a combination of the above. Next, I address the question of what distinguishes the plots alleged by conspiracy theorists from actual conspiracies. I show that conspiracy theories usually imagine far more comprehensive and ambitious – and hence impracticable – plots than actual conspiracies, which are very limited in terms of their scope and objectives. Above all, conspiracy theories assume a false view of people and history in claiming that history can be planned and controlled over any length of time. This leads me to the observation that the term 'conspiracy theory', both in everyday parlance and in academic discourse, is

nearly always an evaluative concept that is used to discredit
the ideas of others – even if they do not display the typical
characteristics of conspiracy theories. That said, it is in my
view nevertheless possible to use the term neutrally, as I
argue in the fourth part of this chapter. Finally, I examine
calls to replace the term 'conspiracy theory' with 'conspiracy
ideology'. This discussion is limited to German-speaking
countries; elsewhere, scholars seem either to have no problem
with it or to accept that the term 'conspiracy theory' is
already so well established that an alternative would fail to
catch on anyway. The debate is, notwithstanding, of general
interest, since it highlights the question of how far conspiracy
theories are in fact theories, and what distinguishes them
from scientific theories.

Characteristics

According to the American political scientist Michael
Barkun, conspiracy theories are characterized – in addition
to the premise of a group of conspirators – by three
basic assumptions: 1) Nothing happens by accident; 2)
Nothing is as it seems; 3) Everything is connected. The
English historian Geoffrey Cubitt, who formulated another
influential definition of conspiracism, takes a very similar
view. For him, intentionality, secrecy (which he refers to
as occultism) and the dualism of good and evil constitute
the essence of conspiracy theory. Intentionality and secrecy
correspond almost exactly to Barkun's first two components
in that the conspirators follow a plan and act in secret, while
dualism is highlighted elsewhere by Barkun. The conspirators
are invariably imagined as evil, and their actions as causing
harm to the wider mass of innocent people.[1]

All these characteristics can indeed be found in Churchill's
short text, especially in the paragraph on 'International
Jews', which I will therefore cite again at greater length:

> In violent opposition to all this sphere of Jewish effort rise
> the schemes of the International Jews. The adherents of this
> sinister confederacy are mostly men reared up among the
> unhappy populations of countries where Jews are persecuted

on account of their race. Most, if not all, of them have forsaken
the faith of their forefathers, and divorced from their minds
all spiritual hopes of the next world. This movement among
the Jews is not new. From the days of Spartacus-Weishaupt
to those of Karl Marx, and down to Trotsky (Russia), Bela
Kun (Hungary), Rosa Luxembourg [sic] (Germany), and
Emma Goldman (United States), this world-wide conspiracy
for the overthrow of civilization and for the reconstitution
of society on the basis of arrested development, of envious
malevolence, and impossible equality, has been steadily
growing. It played, as a modern writer, Mrs Webster, has so
ably shown, a definitely recognizable part in the tragedy of
the French Revolution. It has been the mainspring of every
subversive movement during the Nineteenth Century; and
now at last this band of extraordinary personalities from
the underworld of the great cities of Europe and America
have gripped the Russian people by the hair of their heads
and have become practically the undisputed masters of that
enormous empire.

In a single paragraph, Churchill paints the picture of a global
conspiracy that has been operating at least since 1776, when
the Order of the Illuminati was founded by Adam Weishaupt
– 'Spartacus' to his brethren within the secret society – in
the Bavarian town of Ingolstadt. According to Churchill,
this 'world-wide conspiracy' secretly orchestrated the French
Revolution, was behind various revolutions throughout the
nineteenth century – he is surely thinking in particular of
the series of failed and successful revolutions of 1848 – and
is now, more successfully than ever, orchestrating events in
Russia. Admittedly, Churchill is slightly more careful than
other conspiracy theorists, as he does not entirely disregard
other influences. Still, the conspirators 'played ... a definitely
recognisable part in the tragedy of the French Revolution'
and have 'been the mainspring of every subversive movement
during the Nineteenth Century'. In a manner characteristic of
conspiracy theorizing since the eighteenth century, Churchill
thus considers world history largely the result of a conspiracy.
He denies that the revolutions in different countries were the
result of a number of complex and interrelating factors, some
local, some national, some transnational, and reduces history
to the secret workings of a group of conspirators who are

pursuing a single goal – 'the overthrow of civilization' – and have therefore plotted all of these events.

Moreover, in the short vision of history that Churchill provides here, nothing is as it seems. Not only does he unveil a global conspiracy that has been operating for more than 200 years; without offering any kind of evidence for his claims, he also maintains that Adam Weishaupt, who in reality was raised as a Catholic but later rejected the more traditional versions of religion in favour of Deism, was a Jew, one of those who gave up 'the faith of their forefathers, and divorced from their minds all spiritual hopes of the next world'. In fact, in Churchill's logic, the masterminds behind the various revolutionary efforts he considers are all either Jews who keep their real identities a secret or are controlled by Jews. These explicit and implicit claims allow him to construct a teleological historical narrative that spans from the Illuminati to the Bolshevists, from Ingolstadt to St Petersburg. What we see here in a nutshell, then, is how the characteristics of conspiracy theory identified by Barkun and Cubitt are interconnected. Once one looks beneath the surface of things, the hidden connections become apparent. Admittedly, not everything is connected in Churchill's text – in that regard Barkun exaggerates slightly – but many links between events and people one would not have thought of as related are highlighted.

The dualism of good and evil that Cubitt particularly emphasizes structures Churchill's text in twofold fashion. On the one hand, there is the conflict between the malevolent conspirators, 'schem[ing for] a world-wide communistic State under Jewish domination', and the innocent victims of their plot. On the other hand, there is the conflict that frames Churchill's conspiracy narrative, the conflict between 'Good and Bad Jews', between those subscribing to nationalism and those plotting for international communism. As he claims early in his text, 'The conflict between good and evil which proceeds unceasingly in the breast of man nowhere reaches such an intensity as in the Jewish race.'

When it comes to providing evidence of the alleged plot – a topic I discuss in detail in the next chapter – Churchill's speech is rather untypical. It deviates from what we usually find in conspiracy theory texts in that he does not provide a lot of evidence for his claims. Because of the genre of the text – a short speech that simply does not allow for an in-depth analysis – he does not quote any sources to prove that there really is a plot. In fact, he places the burden of proof on another conspiracy theorist, 'a modern writer, Mrs Webster, [who, he claims] has so ably shown' that the conspirators orchestrated the French Revolution. Such a reference is quite typical of conspiracist discourse, however. Conspiracy theorists often back up their feeble assertions by referring to sources who have made the same claims, usually without offering any convincing evidence themselves. All too often, the conspiracy theorists thus quoted refer back to those who cited them, engaging in a circular logic that creates the impression of serious research and a foundation in facts.

It is no coincidence that Churchill refers to Nesta Webster (1876–1960), a member of the British upper class and wife of Arthur Templer Webster, the Superintendent of the British Police in India. Webster is one of the most significant conspiracy theorists of the twentieth century, whose influence on contemporary conspiracist visions that merge suspicions about secret societies, Jews and communists cannot be overestimated. She single-handedly resuscitated the Illuminati conspiracy theory that had gone out of fashion by the second half of the nineteenth century, and is thus the most important link between late eighteenth- and early nineteenth-century conspiracy theorists like John Robison, Augustin Barruel and Johann August von Starck, who blamed the Illuminati and the Freemasons for the French Revolution, and twentieth- and twenty-first-century writers who do the same.[2]

The book by Webster that Churchill has in mind is *The French Revolution: A Study in Democracy*, from 1919, in which she breathed new life into the allegations of Robison, Barruel and Starck. In the book's epilogue, she also connected the alleged plots around the French Revolution to other revolutions in the nineteenth century and current events in Russia. Still, Webster did not (yet) explicitly argue that the same group of conspirators was behind all of these events. She rather highlighted what she perceived as the overarching structural parallel: all these upheavals were rooted in bottom-up conspiracies. Thus, Churchill is far more extreme in his claims about the reach and longevity of the conspiracy than the source he refers to. However, in subsequent writings Webster caught up with and surpassed Churchill. In *The French Terror and Russian Bolshevism* (1920), *World Revolution: The Plot against Civilization* (1921), *Secret Societies and Subversive Movements* (1924) and a number of other texts, she merged – as the titles of these books already indicate – allegations against Jews, communists, Freemasons and Illuminati far more aggressively. It is tempting to speculate that the way Churchill adopted her argument at least helped to push Webster in that direction.[3]

Typologies

There are conspiracy theories that claim the moon landing was staged in a television studio by the American government, or that the CIA was behind the 9/11 attacks. Others accuse the Illuminati of secretly controlling the destiny of the world for centuries. The Nazis believed that a global Jewish-Bolshevist conspiracy was at work. And in the nineteenth century large numbers of French people believed that the Jesuits were slowly but surely taking control of state institutions. Clearly, not all conspiracy theories are the same. There are significant differences in the scope and degree of advancement of the conspiracy, as well as the nature of the group of conspirators, and it is therefore necessary to introduce a few distinctions at this point. At the same time, we should bear in mind that typologies are heuristic instruments designed to sharpen our awareness of certain phenomena. Needless to say, there will always be hybrid forms that resist precise classification and call into question the choice of categories.

One of the first key distinctions concerns the position in which the conspirators find themselves. Have they already gained control over the institution or country they are plotting against, or indeed over the entire world? Are their plots primarily about consolidating their power or increasing it? Or are they still in the process of assuming that power by infiltrating institutions and subverting society? In other words, is it a 'top-down' conspiracy or a 'bottom-up' one?[4]

The most popular conspiracy theories circulating in Germany between the late eighteenth and mid-twentieth centuries related exclusively to 'bottom-up' plots, as the German historian Johannes Rogalla von Bieberstein has demonstrated. As the subtitle of his book indicates, not only Freemasons and Jews, but also socialists and liberals, were seen as 'conspirators against the social order' who, according to the authorities at the time, had to be prevented at all costs from seizing power.[5] A similar attitude was displayed by the American senator Joseph McCarthy during the 'Red Scare' of the 1950s. Despite claiming to have discovered communists in schools, colleges and the State Department, McCarthy saw the real centres of power – Congress and the White House – as remaining in the hands of 'real', patriotic Americans.

A very different view was taken a hundred years earlier by opponents of the so-called Slave Power Conspiracy. In their eyes, the state was already completely under the control of a conspiracy of radical pro-slavery campaigners who they believed wanted to make the practice compulsory throughout the land. In this case, the conspiracy theorists identified a 'top-down' plot. In 1858, for example, the future president Abraham Lincoln – in one of his most famous speeches, in which he described the USA as a 'house divided' – accused the then president James Buchanan, his predecessor Franklin Pierce, the Supreme Court Chief Justice Roger Taney and the influential congressman Stephen Douglas of heading up a giant conspiracy of slave owners. These conspirators, Lincoln argued, had orchestrated all the crises of recent years in order to achieve their true objective: the introduction of slavery across the whole of the United States.[6]

The distinction between bottom-up and top-down conspiracies is often closely linked to that between 'external' and 'internal' conspiracies. Are the conspirators outsiders who have merely wormed their way into the country or organization they are seeking to undermine? Or have they always belonged to it and simply begun at some point to pursue their own ends instead? External conspiracies almost always tend to be imagined as bottom-up operations, since the state and its key institutions are obviously not yet in the hands of the conspirators. Internal conspiracies, on the other hand, can operate either from the top down or from the bottom up. The government can manipulate the population, and sections of the population can mount secret attempts to seize power. In recent decades, however, there has been a growing tendency in the Western world to identify internal and top-down conspiracies.

One example of a conspiracy theory involving an external, bottom-up plot was the widespread claim in the USA in the 1830s and 1840s that the Pope and the crowned heads of Europe were secretly directing Catholic migration to America. According to many influential Protestant ministers and intellectuals at the time, the ultimate aim was to instigate a takeover that would destroy the shining example of freedom and democracy set by a country that sided with the oppressed masses of Europe and was hence a thorn in the side of absolutist monarchs. In much the same fashion, Iranian president Mahmoud Ahmadinejad consistently blamed all ills, disasters and attacks in his country on US and Israeli plots throughout his eight years in office (2005–13). In both instances, the spectre of an external conspiracy served – consciously or unconsciously – to defuse internal tensions. In most conspiracy theories directed against external adversaries, the nation appears as an organic unit whose real enemies can only come from outside.

The various groups of alleged conspirators mentioned earlier as being feared by nineteenth-century German conservatives are a different story. While they may have been influenced by foreign ideologues, they were not – at least according to the prevailing view – controlled from outside the country. This type of conspiracy was therefore an internal, bottom-up one. The conspiracy scenarios popular in the West in recent decades revolve around internal, top-down conspiracies. As far as the assassination of John F. Kennedy, the moon landing or the 9/11 attacks are concerned, most conspiracy theorists assume the involvement of the US government or at least large parts of it. The tendency to regard the elites of one's own country as conspirators already suggests the close relationship between conspiracy theories and populism, which I discuss in Chapter 4.

Needless to say, categories such as 'top-down' and 'bottom-up' or 'external' and 'internal' are not always as clearly distinguishable in practice as the previous paragraphs perhaps suggest. This is because any assessment of a conspiracy tends to depend on when – i.e. in which phase of its development – we make that assessment. After all, the aim of the conspirators according to all these theories is to achieve power and hold on to it. Thus, the communist conspiracy uncovered by Senator McCarthy is a bottom-up one, since the White House has not yet been conquered. By contrast, the communist conspiracy that Robert W. Welch, the founder of the far-right John Birch Society, claimed to have exposed a few years later in his book *The Politician*, is a top-down one, since President Eisenhower was, in his view, part of the conspiracy; in this case, the conspirators have already taken control of the White House. One reason why the assassination of John F. Kennedy plays such a key role in so many conspiracy theories is that it is viewed by many conspiracy theorists as the tipping point when the conspirators finally took over power and the bottom-up conspiracy became a top-down one. In Churchill's text, on the other hand, the conspirators – typically for the time of writing – have not yet assumed power in Russia, although the originally 'bottom-up' plot is already well advanced outside the UK. Even so, Churchill is ahead of his time in propagating – to use Michael Barkun's terminology – a superconspiracy theory in which various event and systemic conspiracy theories converge.[7]

Event conspiracy theories, as the name implies, centre on a specific, relatively clear-cut event which is claimed to be the result of a plot. The Kennedy assassination, the moon landing, 9/11 or the death of the Polish president Lech Kaczyński when his plane crashed in Smolensk in April 2010 – all these events have given rise to such theories. Systemic conspiracy theories, on the other hand, focus on a particular group of conspirators who are accused of engineering a whole series of events in order to achieve their dark purposes or hold on to power. Such theories have sprung up around groups such as communists, the Illuminati, Jews or the CIA.

Finally, superconspiracy theories are a conglomeration of event and systemic conspiracy theories. The Nazi theory of the global Jewish-Bolshevist conspiracy is a superconspiracy theory because it amalgamates two systemic conspiracy theories, the Jewish one and the communist one. The scenario presented by Robert W. Welch in *The Politician* is quite similar. He traces the global communist conspiracy all the way back to the Illuminati. Even more extreme is the conspiracy theory of the former footballer David Icke, which has many followers, mostly in the English-speaking world. Icke believes that the world is ruled by an elite class of reptiles who landed on Earth from outer space in prehistoric times and feed on the negative energy of human beings. In his view, these extra-terrestrial conspirators are behind almost every event and group around which conspiracy theories are woven. Here we have a particularly striking illustration of the idea that everything is connected. The huge scale involved – something that Welch's and Icke's theories share with those of Churchill and many others – is an important criterion for distinguishing imaginary conspiracies from real ones.

Conspiracy theories and real conspiracies

Up to now, I have omitted to discuss – at least explicitly – the question of whether conspiracy theories are true or not. At the same time, the wording I used at the beginning of this chapter – namely, that conspiracy theories 'assert' the existence of a plot – and, above all, the examples I have chosen so far, point to the fact that I, like the vast majority of academics, view them with a great deal of scepticism. That is not to say, of course, that conspiracies do not occur. From the Catilinarian conspiracy through to the by now widely documented attempt by the Kremlin to influence the 2016 American presidential elections, there have always been secret plots, and it is highly unlikely that this will ever change. But real conspiracies are very different from those that conspiracy theorists claim to have uncovered. And there has never been, to the best of my knowledge, a conspiracy theory as defined in the first part of this chapter that has subsequently turned out to be true.

The first difference between real conspiracies and conspiracy theories concerns the timescale of the alleged plot. According to the extremism expert Armin Pfahl-Traughber, the overwhelming majority of proven conspiracies are 'relatively short-term projects with a concrete objective', such as an assassination or a coup. By contrast, conspiracy theories nearly always posit a 'much larger timeframe of conspiratorial action' associated with far more ambitious but at the same time vaguer objectives ranging through to world domination.[8] Accordingly, in order to achieve their sinister ends, the conspirators – real or imaginary groups such as Jews, communists, Illuminati or aliens – are generally alleged to have committed not just one offence, but a whole series of crimes over a period of years or sometimes decades, and in some cases even over centuries. In such scenarios, the perceived plot thus involves several generations of conspirators.

One might object that this argument disqualifies systemic and superconspiracy theories, but not event conspiracy theories which mostly relate to assassinations or coups or other clearly definable events such as the moon landing. Admittedly, it is easier to imagine such conspiracy theories ultimately turning out to be true. But even leaving aside the fact that most event conspiracy theories soon escalate into bigger scenarios, this is still very, very unlikely, since even event conspiracy theories differ from real conspiracies in one important respect: that of size.

Real conspiracies are generally the work of 'a small group of people',[9] whereas conspiracy theories construct scenarios in which at least dozens, but usually far more people would have to have been involved. A gigantic deception like the staging of the moon landing in a TV studio, or the 9/11 attacks, which unfolded live before the eyes of the world, would require hundreds, if not thousands of insiders and accessories. Against this, critics sometimes contend that, even in the case of an event on the scale of 9/11, it only takes a small number of conspirators acting under false pretences to persuade all the other parties involved – the air defence pilots who failed to intervene, the agents who quickly leapt on the trail of al-Qaida, and many others besides – to do their bidding. But this argument is not conclusive because the involuntary accomplices would discover after the event, if not before, what they had unwittingly helped to engineer, in which case they too would become accessories to the conspiracy.

As the philosopher Brian Keeley argued some twenty years ago, the large number of insiders required by such scenarios militates against the existence of these plots due to the virtual impossibility of keeping them secret.[10] Indeed, the mathematician David Grimes recently went as far as to develop a model to calculate the point at which a given conspiracy would logically become public on grounds of size alone. According to his calculation, the staging of the moon landing could only have been concealed for a maximum of four years.[11] This may be more of a mathematical exercise than an adequate description of reality, but the fact remains that no one has so far come forward to confess their role in the faking of the moon landing, the assassination of Kennedy or the 9/11 attacks, or to accuse others of making them an unwitting accomplice in those acts. Journalists who have defected from what conspiracy theorists call the 'mainstream media' to the conspiracist camp sometimes complain of having been instrumentalized in order to spread lies, but they invariably fail to provide any evidence for this, or for any specific plot – a further indication that such conspiracy theories belong to the realms of fantasy.

Another argument against the existence of such large-scale conspiracy scenarios is likewise mentioned by Keeley: 'The world as we understand it today is made up of an extremely large number of interacting agents, each with ... its own set of goals.'[12] For a conspiracy to be successful, all parties would have to set aside their own interests and devote themselves entirely to the service of the conspiracy, something which is very unlikely, if not impossible. In his excellent introduction to the logic of conspiracy theories, the social psychologist Jovan Byford develops this idea a little further. According to him, a strong argument against the existence of conspiracies as claimed by conspiracy theorists is that there is in reality not one huge conspiracy but many competing smaller conspiracies. Different groups do not, as conspiracy theorists maintain, act in concert, but pursue different and often contradictory aims. Consequently, there is no single group quietly orchestrating events over a long period of time, but a variety of factions – camps within a government, rival intelligence services within a country, mutually hostile departments within the same intelligence service, and so on – which are all bent on implementing their own agenda, if necessary by conspiratorial means, and which regularly get in each other's way. For this reason, Byford concludes, it is nonsensical to assume that one group could seriously control the destiny of an institution, country or indeed the entire world over many years.[13]

Perhaps the strongest argument against conspiracy theories, however, is that they are rooted in a view of human agency and history that has been radically challenged by the modern social sciences. Conspiracy theories are based on the assumption that human beings can direct the course of history according to their own intentions – in other words, that history is plannable. They credit conspirators with the ability to control the destiny of a country or even the world for years or decades at a time. Indeed, they often understand history as a series of plots by one or various groups. Consequently, they have a fundamentally different view of the world from that of psychology, sociology or political science. According to psychology, the ego is not master in its own house, as Sigmund Freud famously put it; in many cases, we don't know exactly what we do or don't want, and find it accordingly difficult to act on our intentions. But even if we did always know our own desires, we still couldn't achieve them, since social systems – as sociology and political science have shown – have a life of their own and generate effects that no one intended.

Few people have articulated this insight as clearly as Karl Popper. In the second volume of *The Open Society and Its Enemies*, he begins the chapter 'Marx's Method' with a general discussion of why human beings 'are, if anything, the product of life in society rather than its creators'. He does not of course deny that 'the structure of our social environment is man-made in a certain sense', but stresses that this is only part of the story: 'even those [institutions and traditions] which arise as the result of conscious and intentional human actions are, as a rule, *the indirect, the unintended and often the unwanted by-products of such actions*'. The task of the social sciences, he therefore concludes, is to investigate these unintended consequences and, ideally, predict them.[14]

This interpretation of history and society is clearly diametrically opposed to that of conspiracy theorists. Significantly, Popper illustrates his general statements with the example of what he calls 'the *conspiracy theory of society*', in order to

show that conspiracist thinking rests on a false understanding
of social processes:

> Conspiracies occur, it must be admitted. But the striking fact
> which, in spite of their occurrence, disproves the conspiracy
> theory is that few of these conspiracies are ultimately
> successful. *Conspirators rarely consummate their conspiracy.*
> Why is this so? Why do achievements differ so widely from
> aspirations? Because this is usually the case in social life,
> conspiracy or no conspiracy. Social life is not only a trial of
> strength between opposing groups – it is action within a more
> or less resilient or brittle framework of institutions and tradi-
> tions and it creates – apart from any conscious counter-action
> – many unforeseen reactions in this framework, some of them
> perhaps even unforeseeable.[15]

Popper's theoretical deliberations are borne out by history.
Wherever a conspiracy enjoyed initial success, it invariably
also had consequences that were in no way intended by
the conspirators. For instance, the murder of Julius Caesar
did not secure the continuation of the Roman Republic,
but led instead to the Empire. The same could be said of
'Operation Ajax', in which the CIA and the British foreign
intelligence service MI6 overthrew the Iranian Prime Minister
Mohammad Mosaddegh in 1953 after he nationalized the
country's oil production. The coup immediately led to an
Islamization of Iranian society, which eventually resulted in
the revolution of 1979. The emergence of an anti-American
religious regime was probably the last thing the Western
conspirators had in mind. Thus, the experience of actual
conspiracies shows that history is often impossible to plan
even in the short term, let alone beyond.

For all the above reasons, no conspiracy theory has ever
turned out in retrospect to be correct. However much this is
claimed, it has never actually happened in the sense that a
theory initially believed by many to belong to the realm of
fantasy has subsequently been proven true. The assumptions
of conspiracy theorists in terms of size and scope alone make
this impossible. Thus, while it is perfectly conceivable that
it will one day be proven beyond all doubt that a second
gunman and others were involved in the assassination of
John F. Kennedy, such a straightforward scenario will never

be enough to satisfy the conspiracy theorists. Instead, they postulate links to the highest levels of the CIA, government, the mafia, exiled Cubans – even Freemasons and the extra-terrestrials who allegedly also built the pyramids.[16] The conspiracist tendency to link together disparate phenomena leads to assumptions that defy all probability.

Another example often cited in support of the claim that many conspiracy theories later turn out to be true is Watergate. Before the first arrests were made in that case, however, there were no suspicions at all, that is to say, no theories, surrounding Nixon or his staff. And once the inquiry was underway, all parties – from the members of the Senate Committee investigating the affair to the investigative journalists Bob Woodward and Carl Bernstein – were extremely careful not to voice suspicions that could not be proven. The well-documented revelations concerning this scandal are therefore a world apart from the still unproven claims of conspiracy theorists that the official version of events was either just the tip of the iceberg or a clever diversionary tactic. They connected Nixon with the mafia, saw him as the victim of a CIA plot, and regarded the whole thing as just one piece in a superconspiracy puzzle encompassing practically every event in recent American history.[17]

The Watergate affair thus provides further confirmation that the extensive scenarios put forward by conspiracy theorists are inconsistent with reality. If the American president – commonly dubbed the most powerful man in the world – cannot even spy on his political opponents at their party offices without it becoming public and leading to his eventual resignation, how can anyone be supposed capable of faking the moon landing, 9/11 or the refugee crisis and keeping it secret for years or even decades? Hence, conspiracy theories are indeed usually wrong. Any account of events that deems everything to be planned and leaves no room for chance, contingency and structural effects cannot adequately comprehend reality. Thus, as Quassim Cassam puts it, 'Conspiracy Theories are implausible by design.'[18]

The term as a means of delegitimization

As we have seen, the term 'conspiracy theory' refers to a specific understanding of the world that assumes that everything has been planned, that everything is connected and that nothing is as it seems. At the same time, when people call something a conspiracy theory, they usually imply that it is wrong. The label thus denotes a set of specific characteristics, and it entails an evaluation. This duality has been inherent in the term since Karl Popper first used it in its modern sense. As Andrew McKenzie-McHarg has shown, the expression 'conspiracy theory' already existed in the late nineteenth century, but had a different meaning until Popper's *The Open Society and Its Enemies*.[19] Initially, a conspiracy theory was – along with suicide or murder theories – one of the possibilities considered by investigators whenever a body was found and the cause of death was unclear. In this context, the term simply meant that it was deemed conceivable that the victim had been murdered by more than one perpetrator, thus fulfilling the legal definition of a conspiracy. Since Popper's openly derogatory statements on the '*conspiracy theory of society*', however, it has been used to refer to the large-scale scenarios discussed above, in order to both capture their characteristics and to suggest that they are without substance. Thus, as Peter Knight stresses, 'The term "conspiracy theory" often acts as an insult itself ... Calling something a conspiracy theory is not infrequently enough to end discussion.'[20]

Consequently, it is always other people who articulate 'conspiracy theories'. Nobody is more aware of the stigma attached to the term than those to whom it is most usually applied. Occasionally, they react by appropriating the concept and claiming that those branded conspiracy theorists by the mainstream are the truly enlightened ones. Or they may avoid it when it comes to their own suspicions, yet use it to discredit allegations directed against themselves or those who share their world view. This tactic is known as *reverse labelling*. You use the same label that others seek to pin on you, dismissing their accusations as conspiracy theories while at the same time presenting your own suspicions as justified and all but proven. 'Who is the one spreading conspiracy theories here?', the former German newsreader Eva Herman asks rhetorically in an article on the refugee crisis which draws on the conspiracy theory of the 'Great Replacement', i.e. the idea that an international financial elite is engaged in a plot to replace Europe's Christian population with a Muslim one. To her and those who believe her, the answer to her question is of course obvious: the puppet politicians and the lying press are spreading conspiracy theories, while she is telling the truth.[21]

Similarly, the authors and commentators on the right-wing populist American website breitbart.com, whose former editor-in-chief Steve Bannon was one of President Trump's top advisers for a time, have attempted ever since Trump's election to dismiss as a conspiracy theory the well-founded suspicion that the Kremlin sought to influence the polls. At the same time, however, the site produces an endless stream of accusations of its own which others would call conspiracy theories. Users commenting on, for instance, an article of 12 December 2016 about the Russia affair agreed with the author that the whole thing was a conspiracy theory put about by the Democrats, yet many of them promptly went on to make counter-accusations – naturally without applying the term to their own case. Comments included an urgent call for Trump to investigate the billionaire George Soros, accusing him of undermining democracy in the USA with his '187 radical organizations'.[22]

Given its negative associations, it is hardly surprising that there is a conspiracy theory about the term 'conspiracy theory'. If you google 'origin term conspiracy theory', you will find precious little about Karl Popper, but countless pages claiming that the CIA invented the term to discredit those who doubt the official version of the Kennedy assassination. Again and again, CIA memo 1035–960 from 1967 is cited by way of evidence. Contrary to common claims, however, this memo was not made public only recently, but as early as 1976, as can be gleaned from the document itself. And more importantly, the memo does not prove the theory about the term's invention. It merely provides arguments refuting the conspiracy theories – already popular at the time – surrounding the Kennedy assassination. The document states that 'Conspiracy theories have frequently thrown suspicion on our organization', and goes on to say:

'The aim of this dispatch is to provide material countering and discrediting the claims of the conspiracy theorists.' However problematic we may find this, the use of the terms 'conspiracy theories' and 'conspiracy theorists' without further definition or explanation shows they were obviously already in everyday use when the memo was written, and not coined by its authors.[23]

Even if the term 'conspiracy theory' was not invented in order to discredit undesirable alternative versions of events, there is nevertheless no doubt that this is one of its main functions in everyday speech. In his book *Conspiracy Panics* (*Conspiracy* Theory *Panics* would have been a more appropriate title), Jack Bratich therefore rejects the rationale of most academics – which I too espouse in this book – and calls for an alternative approach. For Bratich, the concept of the conspiracy theory is not characterized by the duality between definable characteristics that allow a neutral use of the term, and stigmatization, which stands in the way of such a use. To him, it is purely and simply a means of stigmatization and thus delegitimization.[24]

Bratich is strongly influenced by Michel Foucault's idea that power generates knowledge and not vice versa, since it is ultimately those in positions of power who determine what does or does not constitute knowledge. Therefore, Bratich argues, it is impossible to determine on the basis of identifying characteristics – a group acting in secret, an evil plan, etc. – what a conspiracy theory is or is not. Rather, the term is used in common parlance as a way of discrediting a certain idea: 'In other words, the question is no longer, "what is a conspiracy theory?" but "what counts as a conspiracy theory?"' According to Bratich, the term is a weapon used to denounce certain views as illegitimate and false. No more, but also no less.[25]

It is true that ideas are often vilified as conspiracy theories even if they don't have any of the characteristics described at the beginning of this chapter. Not every opponent of vaccination is a conspiracy theorist in the sense that I have used the term so far. That label should only be applied to those who believe that there are forces seeking to conceal the fatal consequences of vaccination from the public, or even to use it to manipulate or subdue the population. All too often, however, the term is used indiscriminately to denigrate anyone with a critical attitude to vaccination.

Conversely, there are ideas and claims which exhibit the characteristics of a conspiracy theory, but are not described as such – at least not initially – because those who promote them are powerful enough to control the discourse on the subject in question. One fateful example from the recent past was the claim by the Bush administration that Saddam Hussein was allied with Osama bin Laden and that the two intended to act in concert to damage the USA. This may sound absurd in hindsight, but in 2003 a significant proportion of the US population genuinely believed it. The claim helped to legitimize the invasion of Iraq. And there is no doubt that it fits the definition of a conspiracy theory: it asserts that two evildoers – Saddam and Osama – and their underlings secretly collaborated in the pursuit of a deadly plan; in so doing, it links together disparate phenomena whose connection is not apparent to the neutral observer. Moreover, the claim was – as events were to prove – untrue.[26]

The example of the Iraq War also points to a problem in Bratich's argument. He assumes that any phenomenon labelled a conspiracy theory always contradicts an official version. He is not alone in this: many scholars, including those who have no quarrel with the concept of the 'conspiracy theory', take a similar view. And it is true that most conspiracy theories advanced in the Western world in recent decades have been directed against an official narrative, that is, one that is subscribed to by elites, the media and the majority of the population. Yet for a time, the Bush administration's claim that Saddam Hussein was secretly in cahoots with al-Qaida was itself the official version in the USA. And in other cultures, such as Eastern Europe and the Arab world, conspiracist suspicions are regularly voiced by elites and the established media. Indeed, many of the above examples show that, historically speaking, the idea that most conspiracy theories are directed against an official version is not borne out for Europe or North America either. There too, the claim that the state was threatened by a major plot was, until the middle of the twentieth century, often the official story.[27]

If we argue historically, a second problem comes into focus. According to the logic of Bratich's strictly Foucauldian approach, conspiracy theories have only existed for as long as the term has been used in its modern sense, i.e. since the mid-twentieth century. If this is the case, what do we make of the obvious 'conspiracy claims' of past centuries? What about texts such as Samuel Morse's anti-Catholic pamphlet *Foreign Conspiracy against the Liberties of the United States*, which, like countless other examples from the eighteenth, nineteenth and early twentieth centuries, offers far more than vague suspicions? This tract describes the alleged conspiracy in detail over hundreds of pages, supplies a wealth of 'evidence', and has many rhetorical, structural and ideological similarities with twenty-first-century books and videos such as the *Loose Change* films or David Ray Griffin's *The New Pearl Harbor*, both of which accuse the Bush administration of being behind the 9/11 attacks. Do we not lose more than we gain if we refuse to regard such a text as the articulation of a conspiracy theory?

For all of Bratich's justifiable scepticism vis-à-vis the term 'conspiracy theory', its use does not have to be confined to the disqualification of unpopular claims. The term can still be used in a relatively neutral sense, since it is possible – as I have shown – to formulate criteria for deciding when it is and is not appropriate. The fact that it is often misused does not invalidate its use per se. And such a neutral use is even possible if one assumes, as I do, that conspiracy theories are usually false. In fact, many scholars across all disciplines are sceptical about the truth claims of the people and narratives they study – take, for example, scholars of religion, anthropologists or historians who study what previous ages regarded as valid knowledge.

Indeed, it is often precisely this sceptical attitude that allows scholars to identify the social causes and effects of the phenomena they are interested in. Had the historians Paul Boyer and Stephen Nissenbaum believed in the existence of witches, they would never have succeeded in demonstrating that the infamous witch trials of 1692 were triggered by an economic conflict in Salem Village.[28] Whether we are dealing with witchcraft or conspiracy theories, it is crucial not to devalue or even pathologize the ideas in question. Nor should we make hasty generalizations about a 'natural' link between conspiracist thinking and political extremism or a tendency towards violence. The fact that such assumptions about conspiracy theories are, unfortunately, still made, not just in everyday discourse but also occasionally by academics, should oblige scholars to take extra care when using the term; it does not, however, make it impossible.

Conspiracy theories as theories

Jack Bratich's study is the most theoretically advanced critique of the concept of 'conspiracy theory'. He is by no means the only one keen to dispense with the term, however. Conspiracy theorists themselves reject it because they claim to be revealing the truth and not just spreading some theory or other. They understand the word theory in its conversational sense of 'mere theorizing' as opposed to practical experience and truth. Conversely, some scholars (exclusively German, interestingly enough) reject the term 'conspiracy theory' because, to them, theories are something noble and scientific and thus the very opposite of conspiracy theories. In their view, conspiracy theories use circular rather than systematic arguments and are ultimately irrefutable. For this reason, Armin Pfahl-Traughber prefers the term 'conspiracy ideology', a view shared by historian Wolfgang Wippermann. According to Pfahl-Traughber, this term is more appropriate because conspiracy theories, unlike scientific theories, are 'not capable of being corrected by evidence to the contrary', that is, they are not falsifiable; rather, they are 'entrenched, monocausal and stereotypical attitudes' displaying a 'one-sided fixation'. Furthermore, conspiracy theories do not 'reflect on the appropriateness of their fundamental assumptions' but take them to be an 'unalterable dogma'. Therefore, he concludes that the term 'conspiracy theory' should only be used in quotation marks, and that it is better to speak of 'conspiracy ideologies'.[29]

This would only shift the problem elsewhere, however. Pfahl-Traughber clearly has a very traditional and accordingly narrow definition of ideology in mind, equating it with false consciousness in the Marxist sense. For him, it is possible and desirable to leave the ideology-led 'misunderstanding' of the world behind and progress to an ideology-free understanding

of it. This is at odds with the prevailing view in cultural studies
and the social sciences, however, which holds that there is no
such thing as ideology-free knowledge. Our understanding of
the world is always governed by basic assumptions that we
do not question and are often barely aware of. Consequently,
Pfahl-Traughber's proposal wouldn't solve the problem he
identifies since, for many people, the term 'ideology' does not
have the negative connotations he intends to convey.

Furthermore, although conspiracy theories differ from
scientific theories in many respects, there are nonetheless
certain similarities. The philosopher Karl Hepfer, for instance,
insists that conspiracy theories, like scientific theories, provide
answers to epistemological questions, thus allowing a 'better
understanding of the world'.[30] While this understanding may
be objectively false, in subjective terms conspiracy theories
do what we expect of theories in general: they explain past
events and allow predictions about the future. Thus, in her
earlier-mentioned article on the 'Great Replacement', Eva
Herman prophesies that the events unfolding in Europe, and
especially Germany, will lead to a war between cultures and
religions, native populations and migrants – a conclusion
she derives from the logic of the evil plan and the conflicts
it has allegedly already led to: 'The unrest already occurring
among the various religious cultures paints an ugly picture of
the future.' Churchill is less explicit on this point due to the
brevity of his text. But his words, too, suggest an underlying
fear that, having once secured Russia, the conspirators will
turn to other countries, notably Britain.

Above all, however, the argument that conspiracy theories
differ from scientific ones in that they are not falsifiable is
invalid. Conspiracy theories can of course be disproved;
indeed, it happens all the time. Although the debunking
of such theories is not as popular on the internet as their
formulation, it is by no means rare. And given the obviously
problematic basic assumptions of conspiracist thinking in
terms of its conception of humanity and history, it is often
quite easy to do. The trouble is that the vast majority of
diehard conspiracy theorists refuse to accept even conclusive
counter-evidence. Instead, they ignore it, seek to invalidate
it or even try to turn it into a proof of their suspicions,
as I show in detail in the next chapter, which deals with

the argumentation strategies of conspiracy theorists. The problem in this case is not, therefore, the theory itself, but the behaviour of those who believe in it.

But even this behaviour is by no means so different from that of the proponents of many scientific theories. Inconsistent though it may be with the scientific ideal, in practice even serious academics sometimes have great difficulty in accepting the refutation of their ideas. They too can be positively irrational, clinging to their views even when they fly in the face of the facts. This phenomenon was demonstrated by Thomas Kuhn in the 1960s with reference to the great paradigm shifts in the history of Western science, but it also applies at a lower level, to scientific theories in the narrower sense. Many economists, for example, still hold fast to the notion that subjects behave entirely rationally – something psychologists claim to have disproved long ago. Similarly, social scientists operating along traditional Marxist lines persist in views that researchers subscribing to other schools of thought regard as obsolete. In these debates, each side accuses the other of mistaking reality, and since both parties reach their conclusions from very different positions, they are highly unlikely to be convinced by any argument proceeding from the theoretical foundation of the opposite point of view.

What counts as refuted and what does not is thus – at least to a certain degree – also a matter of opinion. It depends on the underlying assumptions of the parties concerned, and here the divide between scientific disciplines is often as great as that between conspiracy theorists and non-conspiracy theorists. As far as the debate between the latter is concerned, we could say – drawing on Kuhn – that the opposing parties operate within different paradigms. What appears logical to one strikes the other as absurd, and vice versa. The problem with conspiracy theories is not, therefore, that they are wrongly described as theories. There are plenty of arguments in favour of such a description. What is problematic is the fact that these theories are based on assumptions regarding human agency and the dynamic of historical processes that are no longer shared by the modern sciences. This explains both the attraction and the stigma of conspiracy theories today.

2

'Nothing is as it seems', or: How do conspiracy theorists argue?

'At the heart of conspiracy theory', Mark Fenster observes, is 'a gripping, dramatic story'.[1] Conspiracy theories deal with the struggle between good and evil, the conflict between villains acting in secret to manipulate the unsuspecting masses and the few who, having seen through their plot, are doing their utmost to thwart it. For authors and readers, protagonists and public, they are about enlightenment and revelation – and often no less than a whole new outlook on the world. Fiction films and novels usually dramatize this process to exciting effect. In no way can the same be said of nonfiction, however. Anyone who has waded through Augustin Barruel's *Memoirs Illustrating the History of Jacobinism* (1797), in which the Illuminati are alleged to have orchestrated the French Revolution, or Robert Welch's *The Politician* (1963), in which Dwight D. Eisenhower is 'unmasked' as a communist, will know that conspiracist texts are often anything but compelling. The countless works that have attempted to prove all kinds of conspiracies since the eighteenth century usually suppress all the dramatic elements in favour of an arid style accompanied by multiple footnotes, references and appendices. The content of these texts is exciting – at least, for those who are convinced by them – but the presentation is not. If Barruel and Welch manage to set some of their readers' pulses racing, they do so not by sensationalism, but by what those readers perceive to be persuasive arguments.

In this chapter, therefore, I discuss how conspiracy theorists go about convincing their readers of the existence of the conspiracies they claim to have discovered. I begin with the structure and general strategies of conspiracist argumentation, before going on to outline the various forms of evidence important to conspiracist discourse. The way conspiracy theorists argue has remained remarkably consistent since the age of the Enlightenment. In recent decades, however, the transformation of the media and the shift in the status of conspiracy theories from legitimate to illegitimate knowledge have resulted in some changes. In the third part of this chapter, I explore the distinctive features of conspiracy theories that contradict the official explanation of an event, i.e. the version regarded as correct in political and media circles. A lecture by Daniele Ganser, one of the most well-known conspiracy theorists in the German-speaking world, serves as my prime example here. Finally, I turn to the most popular metaphors used in conspiracist texts to describe the conspirators, their victims and those who have discovered the conspiracy.

Structure and strategies of argumentation

Conspiracy theorists always tell their stories backwards. They ask who stands to gain from an event or development in order to identify the agents responsible. They believe in a mechanistic world where there is no room for coincidence, unintended consequences or systemic effects. To them, observable events are the consequences of intentional actions, making it possible and indeed necessary to establish the motives of the actors concerned. 'Cui bono?' ('Who benefits?') is, accordingly, the implicit guiding question of the online documentary *Loose Change* (2005–9), which attempts to prove that the government of George W. Bush was behind the attacks of 11 September 2001. At the end of the 'Final Cut', the voiceover states that the attacks allowed the Bush administration to push through its military and economic agenda at the expense of the population while increasingly curtailing civil rights in the USA. The commentary ends with the words: 'Ask yourself: What's happening? Where are we headed? And would we be here today without 9/11?' These questions are purely rhetorical since, according to conspiracist logic, the Bush government, as the beneficiary of the attacks, must be responsible for them. It cannot be the case, as non-conspiracy theorists would argue, that it simply sought to profit from a situation not of its own making.[2]

This strategy for identifying the perpetrators has barely changed since the eighteenth century. We find it in Barruel's book on the Illuminati (1797) and in Samuel Morse's *Foreign Conspiracy against the Liberties of the United States* (1835), which exposes a Catholic conspiracy, as well as in Joseph McCarthy's *Retreat from Victory* (1951), about the communist infiltration of the USA, and David Ray Griffin's *The New Pearl Harbor* (2004), in which he attributes responsibility for the 9/11 attacks to the Bush administration. Conspiracy theorists almost always know who the culprits are before they begin their investigation. Consequently, their entire argument is geared towards confirming their suspicions. While the revelations are constantly expanded on and partially updated – nowhere more so than in the digital age – the main thrust of the argument never changes. Those identified as guilty at the beginning generally remain so; at most, further culprits may be added. Mark Fenster's assessment of the conspiracist approach hits the nail on the head: 'There may be more to learn – new details, even new developments … – but there would be nothing more to *know*.'[3]

Because conspiracy theories trace major events back to a single decisive cause, namely the conspiracy they claim to have discovered, they are a vast simplification of social reality. Conspiracism reduces a complex and contradictory reality to a Manichean dichotomy of good versus evil. The generally small group of conspirators ultimately responsible for everything that happens is set against the mass of victims who, apart from the enlightened few, have no idea of what is going on. However, this 'political' complexity *reduction* inevitably goes hand in hand with a 'semiotic' complexity *production*. If disparate events are to be traced back to the activities of a small group, then that group's connections to

the events in question have to be proved, as do the means
by which it manipulates or controls other groups. The
assumption that Lee Harvey Oswald acted alone in the assassination of John F. Kennedy is straightforward and simple.
But if we assume that Kennedy was the victim of a large-scale
conspiracy, things become far more complicated. In the worst
case, one would need to prove, as *The Gemstone File* claims
to,that JFK was murdered by a secret elite surrounding
Aristotle Onassis which has controlled the fate of the USA
since the 1930s.[4]

Perhaps precisely because they aspire to revelations which
they hope will bring about a fundamental change in their
audience's understanding of the world, conspiracy theorists
usually seek to present their findings in a scholarly manner.
The similarities between the conspiracist style and academic
conventions were already highlighted by Richard Hofstadter
in his pioneering essay on 'The Paranoid Style', in which
he points to the countless footnotes and appendices that
have characterized conspiracist texts for centuries. Augustin
Barruel's several hundred page long monograph on the true
causes of the French Revolution has one or more footnotes –
some of them very lengthy – on nearly every page. In Robert
Welch's *The Politician*, the actual text consists of 300 pages,
but the endnotes and bibliography run to almost 200 more.
In David Ray Griffin's *The New Pearl Harbor Revisited*
(2008), the revised version of his 9/11 conspiracy theory,
the 250 pages of text are followed by a good eighty pages of
notes.[5]

The quest for scientific rigour also explains the frequency
with which experts are quoted in conspiracist texts or interviewed in documentaries. As in scholarship proper, they
are there to back up the author's case. Their statements are
meant to prove that the ideas presented – however incredible
they may appear at first sight – have not been developed in a
vacuum, but are part of a serious discourse. For this reason,
conspiracy theorists throughout the centuries have emphasized the academic titles and positions of the people they cite.
In the days when conspiracy theories were still considered
official knowledge, this was very easy, as there were enough
genuine authorities spreading conspiracist ideas. Since the
stigmatization of conspiracist knowledge in the Western

world, however – a topic I discuss in Chapter 4 – it has become much harder to find experts who really are seriously engaged in academic discourse and competent in the relevant field.

Consequently, the few established academics who continue to openly deploy conspiracist ideas, or whose statements are at least appropriated for that purpose, rapidly become stars of the scene; they are constantly in demand and their lectures receive many thousands of shares and comments on YouTube. This is true of the American physicist Steven Jones, for instance, who claims that the Twin Towers of the World Trade Center were blown up with nano-thermite, a chemical compound used predominantly by the military; or, in the German-speaking world, the Swiss historian Daniele Ganser, who likewise casts doubt on the official version of 9/11. A slightly different case is that of the now retired American professor David Ray Griffin, who quickly became one of the loudest voices of the 9/11 Truth Movement at the turn of the millennium and who has so far written nearly a dozen conspiracist books on the September 11 attacks and their consequences. In these, he concentrates chiefly on the alleged physical inconsistencies, arguing that the Twin Towers and the smaller World Trade Center 7 building could never have collapsed as a result of aircraft impact or the damage caused by wreckage and fire, and that they must therefore have been blown up. In *The Mysterious Collapse of World Trade Center 7: Why the Final Official Report About 9/11 Is Unscientific and False*, for example, he criticizes the report by the National Institute of Standards and Technology (NIST). Griffin has no special expertise in the field of physics; as a former professor of religious philosophy, his background is in theology. But the title of professor evidently commands such kudos that he was accepted by at least some sections of the public as an authority on the subject.

In order to exploit this effect, conspiracist documentaries usually avoid identifying their interviewees' precise area of expertise. It it is not unusual to see a person labelled on the screen as 'Dr' or 'Prof' speaking about the statics of the World Trade Center even if they happen to be an art historian or philosopher.[6] If the makers of such videos were challenged on this point, they would no doubt argue that they hadn't the least intention of misleading the viewer, and that the interviewees were ordinary people who had made a study of matters such as statics in order to get at the truth. Flashing up their academic credentials, they would say, simply provides an assurance that they have the intellectual capacity to do so.

That argument would be consistent with a trend that has gradually emerged in recent decades. While some conspiracy theorists still defer to experts, others now regard specialist knowledge as less important than in the past. This shift is a further consequence of the stigmatization of conspiracy theories in the second half of the twentieth century. Since most contemporary conspiracy theories contradict the official version of events, they are accordingly sceptical of officially recognized experts and traditional knowledge hierarchies. In fact, they often accuse these experts of deliberately concealing the truth because they are part of – or at least dependent on – the conspiracy themselves. The de-hierarchization of knowledge brought about by the internet (think Wikipedia) has led to a growing mistrust of traditional expertise in recent years. For this reason, many conspiracy theorists nowadays rely largely on the common sense of 'ordinary' people who doubt the official narrative, or they put their own perceptions and experience centre-stage. As Andrew McKenzie-McHarg has recently demonstrated, this shift from the expert to the eyewitness automatically entails a parallel shift from written evidence to a focus on images in conspiracist accounts.[7]

A particularly striking example of this is the video 'Body Double – PROOF!' produced by the user 'Agent S', which has attracted more than a million views on YouTube to date. In this roughly ten-minute film, the maker homes in on a conspiracist rumour concerning Hillary Clinton that was widely disseminated during the 2016 election campaign among supporters of both Bernie Sanders and Donald Trump. According to the rumour, Clinton was seriously ill, and had been replaced by a double in many of her public appearances. This suspicion gained fresh impetus when she collapsed in public at the memorial for 9/11 victims held on 11 September 2016, only to be seen a few hours later leaving her daughter Chelsea's apartment and getting into a car unaided. Clinton's spokeswoman initially stated that she had been suffering from dehydration; later, she reported that Clinton had pneumonia.

This woeful communication policy naturally gave a further boost to the conspiracy theories.[8]

Agent S's video focuses obsessively on the few seconds that Clinton spends outside her daughter's apartment, arguing that the woman in question is not Clinton, but a double. Agent S provides two pieces of evidence for this: firstly, he states that he has suffered from dehydration and pneumonia himself, and that it is impossible to recover in a few hours to the extent that Clinton would have to have done were she the woman in the video. In other words, he cites his own experience in order to prove the deception. Secondly, he claims that the double is clearly younger, with no wrinkles, a lighter build and a different hairstyle. Again, he relies on his own perception in order to expose the alleged fraud. He is his own expert; he needs no other.

Evidence

Whether relying chiefly on expert knowledge or personal experience, conspiracy theorists since the eighteenth century have used the same kinds of evidence to prove the existence and objectives of a secret plot. The best, that is, the strongest, evidence that such theorists can point to is the existence of a renegade – someone previously part of the conspiracy who has insider knowledge and is therefore able to corroborate outsiders' suspicions. What's more – as Richard Hofstadter already noted – the renegade is living proof that, in the struggle between good and evil, there is a chance that good will prevail since members of the conspiracy can be won over to the other side.[9]

As such, renegades feature frequently in the history of conspiracy theories. Almost as often, however, their revelations are invented to bolster the existing prejudices of conspiracy theorists, and therefore need to be treated with caution. This is true of ex-communists such as Louis Budenz, who confirmed the worst fears of US anti-communists during the 'Red Scare' of the 1950s and claimed to know from his own experience that a huge network of sexually degenerate communist agents was seeking to shake the USA to its foundations. It is also true of Maria Monk, who turned up in New York in the 1830s and fuelled fears of a Catholic plot against the USA with her tales of alleged abuse in a Catholic convent in Quebec. While Budenz had at least demonstrably been a member of the communist party, it is not even clear in Monk's case whether she had ever spent time in the convent in question. Either way, her 'awful disclosures', as her 'first-hand account' is entitled, are a forgery, written in reality by a group of Protestant ministers. This demonstrates the tendency of some conspiracy theorists not only to falsify evidence, but to combat a perceived conspiracy by engaging in conspiracy themselves.[10]

Renegades not only serve as guarantors for the claims of others, but often become powerful accusers themselves. Defecting to the 'good' side gives them considerable cultural capital in the eyes of their conspiracy-believing publics, which they can utilize for their own ends. Thus, the German journalists Gerhard Wisnewski and Mathias Bröckers use their former careers in the mainstream media to lend added credibility to their accusations of censorship and manipulation in the industry. The Swiss historian Daniele Ganser regularly presents himself in his lectures as someone who has cast off the shackles of academia in order to be able to continue speaking the truth. And even Donald Trump, who seized on numerous conspiracy theories during his election campaign – especially those representing Hillary Clinton as part of a global conspiracy against the American people – repeatedly cast himself in the role of a renegade. Because he had been part of the elite himself, he knew exactly how they betrayed and exploited ordinary people, he said in an interview with the best-known US conspiracy theorist Alex Jones in December 2015. He repeated this claim at an election rally in Florida in October 2016, which I discuss in more detail in Chapter 5.[11]

Another equally important source of evidence for conspiracy theorists are confidential documents from inside the conspiracy which, once public, are meant to speak for themselves and prove the conspiracy beyond all doubt. Thus, Trump used his speech in Florida to refer to Clinton's email correspondence, which the platform Wikileaks had published a few months previously. According to Trump, these emails were proof of Clinton's central role in a major conspiracy. The same goes for the CIA memo mentioned in the previous chapter, which allegedly demonstrates that the term 'conspiracy theory' was invented by the intelligence service in order to discredit doubters of the official version of Kennedy's assassination. To neutral observers, however, all these cases generally appear to involve gross misjudgements, as the documents give only limited, if any, grounds for conspiracist interpretations – and then only when individual sentences are taken completely out of context.

However, conspiracy theorists through the ages have not only put their own spin on various 'secret' documents, but indeed gone as far as to forge them. The more cynical have done so for strategic reasons, in order to spread conspiracy theories they themselves did not believe in, while genuine believers have been motivated by the need to convince more people. The most famous forgery is, without doubt, *The Protocols of the Elders of Zion*, which claims to document a secret meeting between the leaders of a global Jewish conspiracy to discuss plans for world domination. The origin of the text is still unclear, but we do know that it was first published in 1903 in an obscure Russian newspaper; that large parts of it consist of plagiarized material also found in German and French texts circulated in earlier decades; that the *Protocols* only really became popular after the Russian Revolution; and that they continue to this day to fuel anti-Semitic conspiracy theories around the world – with dire consequences. Tellingly, there are those who know full well that the text is a forgery, but accept it as evidence because they believe it articulates the essence of Judaism.[12]

Not all conspiracy theories hinge on a supposed 'smoking gun', however, and not all conspiracy theorists go to the length of forging evidence in order to prove something they either firmly believe in or wish to propagate for strategic reasons. In other cases, the conspiracy theorist has to interpret the available material or observable events in order to prove the existence of the plot. Here, the mode of inference, i.e. of allegedly logical deduction, is crucial. Invariably, their interpretation is guided by their existing 'knowledge' of who is behind the conspiracy.

A prime example of this mode of reasoning is Abraham Lincoln's famous 'House Divided' speech, delivered to

Republican Party supporters in Springfield, Illinois on 16 June 1858. Only the first few sentences have stuck in the collective cultural memory, namely those where Lincoln indirectly prophesies the Civil War: 'A house divided against itself cannot stand. I believe this government cannot endure, permanently, half slave and half free. I do not expect the Union to be dissolved – I do not expect the house to fall – but I do expect it will cease to be divided. It will become all one thing or all the other.' Less well known, however, is the fact that Lincoln then goes on to develop an elaborate conspiracy theory, claiming that supporters of slavery, known as the 'Slave Power', have already succeeded in bringing the White House, the Supreme Court and Congress under their control, with the aim not only of preserving the practice in the southern states, but of extending it across the USA. Specifically, he accuses the then president James Buchanan, his predecessor Franklin Pierce, the Chief Justice of the Supreme Court, Roger Taney, and the influential congressman Stephen Douglas of orchestrating the events of the previous years so as to bring the Slave Power substantially closer to this goal. Lincoln has no direct evidence for this claim – there is no protocol of a secret meeting – and he therefore has to draw his conclusions from the events themselves. Once again, he uses the metaphor of a house:

> But when we see a lot of framed timbers, different portions of which we know have been gotten out at different times and places and by different workmen – Stephen, Franklin, Roger and James, for instance – and we see these timbers joined together, and see they exactly make the frame of a house or a mill, all the tenons and mortises exactly fitting, and all the lengths and proportions of the different pieces exactly adapted to their respective places, and not a piece too many or too few – not omitting even scaffolding – or, if a single piece be lacking, we see the place in the frame exactly fitted and prepared to yet bring such piece in – in *such* a case, we find it impossible not to believe that Stephen and Franklin and Roger and James all understood one another from the beginning, and all worked upon a common *plan* or *draft* drawn up before the first lick was struck.[13]

Lincoln's assertion that the many and at first sight often contradictory events of the 1850s form a coherent whole leads him to conclude that there must be a conspiracy at work; it is inconceivable that the driving forces behind these events are not in collusion with each other. To him, only the assumption that they are acting according to a common plan can explain what is currently happening in the USA.

Another important element of the conspiracist rationale is that of conclusion by analogy, a technique that allows a conspiracy to be postulated despite the absence of any concrete evidence. Thus, 9/11 conspiracy theorists invariably point to the fact that the Bush administration clearly lied in the lead-up to the Iraq invasion of 2003: Saddam Hussein neither possessed weapons of mass destruction, nor was he secretly in cahoots with Osama bin Laden. From this, they conclude that Bush and his inner circle are also lying about 11 September 2001, that the official version is therefore untrue, and that the attacks must have been a government plot. A similar reasoning has been used in recent years to 'prove' that the USA was behind both the attempted Turkish coup in 2016 and the change of government in Ukraine in 2014. After all – so the argument goes – the Americans have a track record of destabilizing governments and supporting rebels throughout the world.

That said, conspiracy theorists do not always need to go to the trouble of teasing out the 'true' meaning of the evidence, let alone citing analogies. Rather, their arguments oscillate between deep and surface interpretation. Once they have realized that a conspiracy exists, and what its objective is, they can find evidence for it (almost) anywhere. Often, this is because they now know how to read the secret communications of the conspirators. Anyone who is convinced that the secret society of the Illuminati was not dissolved in 1785 as official histories claim, but went underground and continues to direct the fate of the world to this day, will be quick to see pyramid, diamond or devil's horn signs in the hand gestures of public figures, interpreting them as covert messages to fellow conspirators. The internet is teeming with images and videos exposing high-profile personalities as members of the Order of the Illuminati. Virtually all the leading politicians of recent years – from George W. Bush through to Angela Merkel (Fig. 1) and Mahmoud Ahmadinejad – have become targets for such theories. The same goes for artists such as the rapper Jay-Z and his wife, the singer Beyoncé (Fig. 2). Her appearance at the Super Bowl in February 2013 is interpreted by conspiracy theorists as a barely concealed piece of Illuminati propaganda due to her repeated use of the pyramid hand gesture. The fact that some of the floodlights cut out shortly afterwards is attributed to Beyoncé's supernatural powers, in line with the persistent view of the Illuminati as a group in league with the Devil.

The example cited here illustrates both the conspiracy theorist's obsession with details and the specific way in which those details are treated. Very often, a small thing – in this case a random hand gesture or a move in a musical choreography – is taken out of its actual context and placed in a new,

Figure 1. Angela Merkel forms the famous diamond shape with her hands. © Ulrich Baumgarten/Getty Images

conspiracist setting where it takes on a whole new meaning. Thus, the diamond shape that Angela Merkel often makes with her hands is no longer a personal quirk, but a secret sign that can only be read by the initiated. Since the conspiracist world view assumes that everything is connected, the question of whether it is reasonable to interpret details in this way doesn't even arise. Rather, there is no other possible way.

It is not only connections that are flagged up by conspiracy theorists when assembling details from different texts and images, however. Often, they seek to substantiate their arguments by highlighting the differences. Thus, the *Loose Change* films compare the few available images of the spot where a plane hit the Pentagon on 11 September 2001 with images of other plane crashes in order to prove that an aircraft cannot have been the cause. That different types of plane were involved in each case; that they had different amounts of fuel in their tanks and that the explosions were

Figure 2. The US singer Beyoncé during her 2013 Superbowl performance. © Kevin Mazur/WireImage/Getty Images

therefore not all equally powerful; that the pictures were taken from different angles, some of them immediately after the incident, and some during the clean-up operations – none of this is taken into account. When it comes to explaining what else might have struck the Pentagon, the films fail to take a clear position. By comparing photos of the damage to the Pentagon with images of Slobodan Milošević's official residence, however, which was verifiably hit by cruise missiles in 1999, they suggest that it could have been a rocket of this kind. Thus, details from different contexts are integrated – in a sequence of a few minutes – into the filmmaker's own 9/11 narrative. Sometimes the differences are emphasized, sometimes the similarities.

Since it is a premise of conspiracism that nothing happens by chance, every detail is potentially significant to the conspiracy theorist, partly – or even especially – because a non-conspiracist would regard it as irrelevant to the events to which the theory relates. This is as true of Beyoncé's and Merkel's hand gestures as it is of the famous 'umbrella man' who many conspiracy theorists regard as part of the plot against John F. Kennedy. The umbrella man can be seen in the few seconds of footage filmed by Abraham Zapruder on 22 November 1963 – the only moving pictures we have of Kennedy's assassination. Shortly before the shots are fired, the camera captures a man who – moments before Kennedy's limousine drives past him – opens an umbrella and waves it in the air. Because it was a sunny day, and he was the only person in the crowd with an umbrella, conspiracy theorists have concluded that this was a signal to the gunmen (those who regard the umbrella man as part of the plot always assume that there were several) to open fire. The man has, however, been proven to have nothing to do with the assassination, and there is a plausible, if somewhat obscure explanation for his admittedly rather odd behaviour. It goes without saying that hardened conspiracy theorists were unconvinced by this, regarding it as a rather poor attempt at a cover-up.[14]

The strategies discussed so far are encountered to varying degrees in all conspiracist texts from the eighteenth century onwards. With the advent of the internet, however, and the availability of programs that make it easy to produce videos from one's own and borrowed material, the method of argumentation deployed by conspiracy theorists has changed to a certain degree. I look at these developments in detail in Chapter 5, but for now I would like to mention a phenomenon that was particularly popular in the first decade of the twenty-first century (and has since already been replaced by newer digital formats): that of the feature-length documentary. While some conspiracy theorists continued to produce printed texts interpreting written and visual material in the traditional way, others switched from books to this new medium.

As well as relying on the established arguments, these films seek above all to overwhelm their audience. One of the differences between reading a book and watching a film is that reading allows you to go at your own pace. You can pore over individual sentences or re-read them several times, flick back through the pages or take time to examine a printed image in detail. With films, on the other hand, the speed is predetermined, and it is not so easy to go back. In theory, of course, we can press the pause button on a YouTube video or watch a scene multiple times. But that's not the way we normally consume films. And documentaries such as *Loose Change* or Alex Jones's *The Obama Deception* exploit this in their attempt to convince viewers of the alleged conspiracy.

These films are a collage of snippets from news and other TV broadcasts along with animations, graphics, interviews, still images of documents and various other elements. As the narrative builds up to a major revelation, the cutting rate rapidly increases. The viewer is bombarded with details, leaving them no time to properly process or even question what they are seeing. This is compounded by the fact that such documentaries move incredibly fast through time and space. Within a few short seconds, we switch from the Pentagon in 2001 to 1990s Yugoslavia, a plane crash in Greece, a hearing in Congress and back to the Pentagon. The tendency to take details out of context and embed them in new contexts is even greater here than in conspiracist texts. Through aesthetic techniques such as the use of rhythmic montage or a consistent soundtrack throughout a sequence, a certain degree of formal coherence is ensured. This replaces the logical coherence of the argument, which is fed to the viewer so fast that they have virtually no choice but to trust the domineering voiceover. The role of the voiceover is to explain what the viewer is seeing, or is intended to see; to make connections; and to integrate it all into the bigger picture. In the most technically accomplished of these films, this results in a conspiracy narrative that can appear extremely persuasive at first sight (as many of my students would confirm), but which, on closer inspection, is no more capable than conspiracist texts of proving the alleged plot (as my students can also confirm).

Countering the official version

As shown in Chapter 1, conspiracy theories do not necessarily always contradict an official version of events. Historically speaking, they usually *were* the official version, and in many parts of the world they still are. In Europe and the USA, however, conspiracy theories have been stigmatized for some decades. Consequently, the dominant form of conspiracy theory here is one that presents an alternative to the version communicated by the government and the media. The arguments deployed by conspiracy theories that challenge an existing explanation have a number of characteristic features that distinguish them from others.

Theories of this kind claim to offer the better explanation because they go further than the official version. They resolve contradictions which the official version is forced to accept because it can offer no explanation for them apart from the general intractability of reality. Scientists know that even laboratory experiments occasionally generate results that do not fit the rest of the data. But they also know that such 'errant data' can be safely ignored if enough other factors point in a particular direction. For conspiracy theorists, on the other hand, such 'errant data' become the basis of their whole argument. Because there is no room for chance or contradictions in their world view, there must be something else behind these incongruities.

The errant data employed by conspiracy theorists can be divided into two categories. Firstly, there are details and incidents that are genuinely impossible or difficult to reconcile with the official narrative. For instance, there is no good explanation as to why more than 10 per cent of nearly 200 witnesses to the Kennedy assassination claimed to have heard more than the three shots Lee Harvey Oswald was proven to have fired. It also remains a mystery why Timothy McVeigh – who carried out the 1995 attack on the Murrah Federal Building in Oklahoma City and, according to the security services, planned the operation in minute detail – fled the scene in a car with no licence plate and was consequently arrested within two hours following a routine police check. But such logical and psychological inconsistencies are not signs of a conspiracy, as the philosopher Brian Keeley, one of the first people to study this phenomenon, stresses: 'What conspiracy theories get wrong ... is that the existence of errant data alone is not a significant problem with a theory' but is to be expected given 'the imperfect nature of our human understanding of the world'.[15] Moreover, conspiracy theories produce their own errant data, which they tend to ignore completely. For example, almost 90 per cent of those who witnessed the Kennedy assassination heard only three shots. Their testimony thus corroborates the official explanation and contradicts the conspiracist ones.

The other category of errant data is that presented by conspiracy theorists as absolutely inexplicable without the assumption of a plot, but which, on closer examination, turns out to have a perfectly rational explanation. Thus, conspiracy theorists consistently point to the fact that the passport of Satam al-Suqami, one of the 9/11 attackers, was found on the pavement in the vicinity of the World Trade Center. Daniele Ganser, for example, to whom I devote a case study below, often presents a collage in his lectures featuring a bird's-eye view of the completely devastated World Trade Center site in the background, and a photo of al-Suqami's passport in the foreground. The implication is clear: given that it was surely impossible to find anything among this pile of wreckage, the passport must have been planted. At this point, there is usually a loud, indignant laugh from the audience. Presented thus, the 'discovery' of the passport becomes a form of errant data proving that the official version cannot be true.

However, it is only the presentation that turns it into errant data, and this is all too often the case when conspiracy theorists place errant data at the heart of their argumentation. What Ganser neglects to mention is that the passport was found prior to the collapse of the towers, that is, when there was virtually no devastation on the ground. Nor does he mention that other passengers' passports were also found, along with other items from the plane, which are exhibited in the 9/11 Memorial Museum. A closer look, then, reveals the errant data to be illusory.

Such counter-narratives are similarly dismissive of expert opinions from the other side. To 9/11 conspiracy theorists, the numerous experts who have explained in a series of official reports or in the media why the impact of the planes caused the Twin Towers to collapse and why the smaller subsidiary building, World Trade Center 7, collapsed a few hours later, are not credible. They are lying, either because they have come under pressure from the conspirators – or are even part of the conspiracy themselves – or because their blind faith in the official version leads them to deny reality. Conversely, the few physicists and architects who argue that the buildings must have been blown up are celebrated for their determination to tell the truth in the face of intimidation. Thus, the statements of both camps are turned into evidence of the conspiracy.

Similarly, conspiracy theorists refuse to accept that, in emergency situations like that of September 11, false reports can emerge which spread like wildfire at first, only to be revised shortly afterwards. Almost every conspiracist video documentary on 9/11 features clips from live American TV coverage in which either survivors or reporters claim that explosions could be heard inside the World Trade Center buildings. It does not occur to conspiracy theorists that this could be the result of misperceptions or rumours that readily arise amid the general confusion and panic, and which were then picked up by the media in order to supply an audience hungry for information. To the conspiracy theorists, these reports represent a moment of truth before the 'synchronization' of the media by the conspirators. As such, they are further evidence that the buildings were blown up.

A specific kind of false reporting that conspiracy theorists are particularly interested in is that which can be claimed to indicate that somebody knew in advance what was going to happen. Such foreknowledge is regarded by conspiracy theorists as powerful evidence of the existence of a plot. Thus, countless 9/11 documentaries point out that the BBC reported the collapse of the WTC 7 building twenty minutes too soon – when the building was still standing. This false intelligence presumably arose because the security forces already feared at that point that the building would collapse, and the information came through distortedly to Reuters, the news agency used by the BBC. To the conspiracy theorists, however, the early announcement is a sign that both the events and the responses to them were precisely planned, until an error occurred that brought the plot to light.

Sometimes, a simple slip of the tongue can be taken as evidence of a conspiracy theory. During the evening of 11 September 2016, a few hours after Hillary Clinton collapsed at the memorial for the victims of 9/11, an ABC presenter opened a news broadcast with the words: 'We begin with the breaking news about Hillary Clinton's death.' His next sentence was: 'Hillary Clinton's doctor has just revealed the presidential candidate has been diagnosed with pneumonia.' This was followed by a report on her state of health, but the damage was already done. Countless YouTube videos homed in on these few seconds, casting doubt on the official explanation that the presenter had made a harmless slip. Instead, they linked it to the rumours surrounding Clinton's health and her double, thus fanning the flames of conspiracism. A member of Alex Jones's team speculated in a short clip that the broadcaster had accidentally 'reported something that wasn't supposed to be reported yet', thereby hinting at a large-scale plot. In Germany, the former journalist Gerhard Wisnewski used the mistake to 'prove' in a video that Hillary Clinton, although not dead, was nevertheless suffering from Parkinson's.[16]

For some conspiracy theorists, this practice of pointing out alleged contradictions and errors in the official version of events is merely a first step towards an explicitly articulated alternative explanation. Other conspiracy theorists concentrate chiefly on exposing the perceived inconsistencies, and only develop their own version implicitly. This strategy has become particularly common in recent decades, and renders conspiracy theorists less vulnerable to attack in a number of ways. For one thing, it obviates the need to name the real culprits, something that is usually much trickier than simply sowing doubts about the official narrative. A welcome side-effect of this vagueness – particularly for those who earn money from disseminating their theories and therefore depend on a wide audience – is that it makes their product attractive to more people. If it is left open whether Bush, Cheney and Rumsfeld were behind the attacks of 9/11 or whether they were carried out by the military without their knowledge, people of either persuasion will feel vindicated because they can fill in the gaps in the text according to their own belief.

Another advantage of concentrating on the supposed contradictions in the official version is that the person concerned can reject the label 'conspiracy theorist': after all, they are not expounding a theory, but merely posing questions. As Mathias Bröckers and Christian C. Walther write in their foreword to *11.9. Zehn Jahre danach: Der Einsturz eines Lügengebäudes* (9/11 Ten Years On: The Collapse of a House of Lies), 'We, as freelance authors and attentive observers, can ... point to what needs investigating in connection with 9/11, which witnesses should be heard under oath, which studies and expert reports commissioned, and which files and documents examined.' They want their book to be understood merely as 'a catalogue of the worst omissions, crassest inconsistencies and most glaring contradictions in the official version of events', insisting that: 'We have no theory to offer, let alone a conspiracy theory, but we can prove that the official version of events is a conspiracy theory.'[17]

In the vast majority of cases, however, this open-endedness is, as Jovan Byford has demonstrated, disingenuous, if not deceitful. For although conspiracy theorists insist that they are only pointing to alternative explanations, they nearly always show a clear bias towards the conspiracist explanation, without ever making this explicit. The same is true of Bröckers and Walther. From the book's subtitle, 'The collapse of a house of lies', to that of the epilogue, 'A memorial to Dick and Don', referring to the then Vice-President Dick Cheney and Secretary of Defense Donald Rumsfeld, the authors consistently suggest – with varying degrees of subtlety – that the US government itself is the ultimate author of the attacks. Although the rhetoric and argumentation strategies of this and countless other books differ from those of Barruel, Morse or McCarthy, the end result is nonetheless a conspiracy theory.[18]

Case study: Daniele Ganser

Someone who has perfected this technique of supposedly 'just asking questions' is Daniele Ganser, one of the most famous and successful conspiracy theorists in the German-speaking world. Ganser vehemently rejects the label 'conspiracy theorist' and claims to pose the uncomfortable questions that other scholars don't dare to ask for fear of damaging their careers. Superficially at least, his own back story does lend this stance a certain credibility. Ganser was awarded a doctorate by the History Department of the University of Basel in 2001 for a dissertation on the paramilitary group 'Gladio'. 'Gladio' was a so-called stay-behind organization designed to carry out acts of sabotage behind enemy lines in the event of an invasion by the Warsaw Pact troops. Although this dissertation already shows signs of conspiracist thinking, as several experts have highlighted in reviews of the book, it made Ganser famous and paved the way for his academic career. He lectured first at the ETH Zürich (Swiss Federal Institute of Technology), then at the University of Basel, while working on a postdoctoral thesis. He lost both posts, however, due to the increasingly conspiracist stance he adopted from 2005 onwards vis-à-vis the official version of the 9/11 attacks. In 2011, he went freelance and founded the Swiss Institute for Peace and Energy Research (SIPER), and has since made a living from his publishing and lecturing activities.[19] To this day, many of Ganser's lectures still focus on 9/11. He repeatedly insists that he doesn't know what happened on 11 September 2001 either, but that it is important to find out. If we look closer at the numerous lectures available on the web, however, it soon becomes clear given my previous remarks that he absolutely can be described as a conspiracy theorist, since he does more than just ask questions.

In December 2014, Ganser addressed a packed lecture hall at the University of Tübingen on the subject of 'The terrorist attacks of 11 September 2001 and the "clash of civilizations": why peace studies should challenge the enemy stereotypes portrayed in the media'. The lecture was filmed and posted online with English subtitles by the former radio host Ken Jebsen, who has run the alternative news channel KenFM – a popular forum for German-speaking conspiracy theorists – for many years. To date, it has attracted more than 1,100,000 views. In it, Ganser shows himself to be an eloquent and charismatic speaker who can also be very witty at times. His timing and punchlines, and above all his calm style and precise turn of phrase set him apart from the common run of conspiracy theorists, who tend to be much more emotional and less polished. Ganser always speaks without notes, accompanied by professionally produced PowerPoint presentations.

This alone lends him a certain authority, which he also asserts quite explicitly by persistently emphasizing his role as an academic, and hence an expert on the subject. He often uses the phrase 'we historians', thereby positioning himself as part of a community that can legitimately claim for itself the right to pronounce on events such as 9/11. At the same time, he also repeatedly distances himself from that community by insisting that – unlike him – the general mass of historians shy away from asking questions about 9/11. Towards the end of the video, he even shows a photograph of his doctoral oath, committing him to 'discover and spread the truth'. In this way, he presents himself as independent and uncompromising, a 'genuine' scholar (in contrast to the rest) who – as he is also at pains to emphasize – has been penalized for his tenacity by being excluded from the academic community and branded a 'conspiracy theorist'.

Here we have an example of how the stigmatized status of the conspiracy theorist can be turned into an advantage, enhancing their credibility and authority in the eyes of 'their' public. In the video, this is clear from the way Ganser's audience responds to his self-positioning. While the audience at a 'normal' academic lecture would most likely roll their eyes at such talk, Ganser's tale of how he quit his job at the university rather than give up his quest for the truth earns a spontaneous round of applause.

In terms of argumentation, Ganser uses many of the strategies described in this chapter, but he does so more indirectly than most other conspiracy theorists. Although his statements are built around the same question of 'Cui bono?', he never poses it explicitly. The substance of his insinuations, however, is that the American government was behind the 9/11 attacks because it needed a pretext to carry out its long-planned invasion of Iraq and so gain access to the country's oil reserves. Thus, Ganser begins with the West's dependence on oil and gas, emphasizing that the majority of these resources are concentrated in the Gulf region and hence in Muslim states. Later, he shows a clip from the plainly conspiracist documentary *The New American Century*, which can also be found on YouTube. This film identifies the group of neocons, i.e. the new conservatives around Vice-President Dick Cheney and Secretary of Defense Donald Rumsfeld, as the masterminds of the conspiracy, with President Bush merely a puppet of the regime.

The excerpt Ganser shows his audience ends with a document that features in every 9/11 conspiracy: the strategy paper of the neoconservative think-tank 'Project for a New American Century', to which Cheney and Rumsfeld belonged along with Rumsfeld's deputy Paul Wolfowitz and security adviser Richard Perle. In this report, published in September 2000 – a year before the attacks – the group argues not only for a stronger military presence in the Middle East in order to better represent US national interests there, but also for an expansion of the military in general. The report recognizes, however – and these are the closing quotations of the film, before Ganser himself takes the floor again – that the proposed process would take a long time unless some catastrophic event, such as a 'new Pearl Harbor', were to accelerate its progress. Ganser takes up this point directly, explaining that, after 9/11, a number of researchers questioned whether there was a connection between the strategy paper and the attacks: 'What is the correlation here? Is this a new Pearl Harbor?'

This is clever, but also highly manipulative, as Ganser is twisting the facts. True, many scholars have emphasized the parallels between 9/11 and Pearl Harbor, and the topic also featured prominently in public discourse after the event, especially during the first few years. But there has never been any serious scholarly inquiry into whether the neocons in the administration were behind the attacks. And yet this is precisely what Ganser suggests early on in the lecture by making a link between the strategy paper and the attacks and claiming that other academics have done the same. He thus uses the typical conspiracist structure of argumentation according to which, once the culprits have been identified, the evidence will automatically follow. Having once embraced the suspicion that the neocons were responsible, we can find freely available documents to support it. This conclusion is particularly likely to suggest itself to those among Ganser's audience who accept – or at least do not rule out – the claim of another well-known conspiracy theory: namely, that the Roosevelt administration knew of the impending attack on Pearl Harbor, but allowed it to happen in order to compel an isolationist nation to enter the Second World War.

That Ganser is intentionally invoking Pearl Harbor conspiracy theories here is also evident from his directly subsequent remark that there are three different versions of what happened on September 11: the official version; the theory that the government did not carry out the attacks itself, but knew of the plans and allowed the attackers to go ahead because it suited its purposes to do so; and the theory that the government itself was responsible for the attacks. Ganser presents these three explanations as equally valid hypotheses, and later describes all three as conspiracy theories, since each assumes the involvement of more than one person. What he doesn't mention is that the official version differs significantly from the other two in its objectives and scope. This is because he wants to discredit the official version and legitimize the others, though he doesn't say so directly, of course. Instead, he declares himself unable to 'solve for you today' the question of which is correct: 'Not because I don't want to, but because I don't know myself. But I am fighting to make it possible to speak openly of these three accounts.' Here, Ganser is presenting himself as someone who, rather than spreading conspiracy theories, simply asks questions with the aim of stimulating impartial debate.

It soon becomes clear which reading he prefers, however – and, once again, without his having to spell it out. Ganser has just made the point that only those researchers who promote the official version have any chance of an academic career. And, as the majority of his audience will most likely have known (or gathered from the introduction to his lecture, which is unfortunately not included in the video), Ganser has indeed been denied such a career. The message he is indirectly communicating here becomes even clearer in the next part of the lecture. Immediately after presenting the three versions, Ganser shows the audience a photograph of the Bush administration, featuring Bush, Cheney and Rumsfeld along with Secretary of State Colin Powell, National Security Advisor Condoleezza Rice and CIA Director George Tenet. He then makes the following comment: 'Someone once said to me: "After looking at this picture for a while I got the impression I was looking at a picture of the mafia."' Again, Ganser is careful to attribute the words to someone else. But the implication is the same: the Bush administration is a collection of criminals. Ganser then goes on to reinforce this idea by briefly revisiting the patently false information and lies circulated in the lead-up to the invasion of Iraq, notably the claim that Iraq possessed weapons of mass destruction. His subtext is clear: if the government lied on that count, it is bound to be concealing the truth elsewhere. What we have here, then, is an example of the previously mentioned 'conclusion by analogy' technique so popular with conspiracy theorists.

After digressing into oil wars and Islam for a while, Ganser finally returns to the 9/11 attacks. Like many conspiracy theorists, he now concentrates on the collapse of WTC 7, a much smaller skyscraper that stood next to the Twin Towers and collapsed in the afternoon of September 11 even though it had not been hit by a plane. According to the official explanation, the fire from the Twin Towers had spread to the building, and it was this that ultimately caused its collapse. Ganser relates how this explanation had bothered him from the start, and how his doubts had become overwhelming when the report published by the 9/11 Commission in 2004 failed to mention WTC 7. Here, he uses the typical conspiracist argument that the omission of a matter considered by conspiracy theorists to be important is in itself evidence of a plot. What he fails to mention, however, is that the report gives no more space to the collapse of the other buildings – and that there is nothing remotely surprising in this. The task of the Commission was, after all, to investigate the security loopholes that made the attacks possible. Which building collapsed when and for what reason was not relevant in that context.

To doubters of the official version of events, however, this question is extremely important. It is a cornerstone of many 9/11 conspiracy theories that the collapse of WTC 7 could never have been caused by fire alone. Ganser quotes a structural engineer from the ETH Zürich, according to whom the building was 'in all probability demolished'. He then shows a video recording of the collapse of WTC 7 and draws his audience's attention to the 'corners' of the building, which all collapse at the same time – a clear indication of a detonation, according to the engineer. From the images, it does indeed look to the impartial eye like the building was blown up, and many experts were surprised that it should have collapsed. Ganser does not show his audience the full version of the video, however, from which it is plain that the collapse was by no means symmetrical and lasted not merely seven but about nineteen seconds. Nor does he show any of the videos taken from the other side of the building, which reveal how badly damaged it already was.

Instead, he mentions a report of 2002 by the US Federal Emergency Management Agency (FEMA) which stated that it did not yet know exactly how the fires inside the building had led to its collapse. Initially, therefore, this was a classic case of errant data that were considered irrelevant to the explanation of the event as a whole. As it happens, the National Institute of Standards and Technology (NIST) did in fact publish a report in 2008 explaining how the fire caused the collapse and how the damage the building had suffered resulted in a free fall of about 2.25 seconds. Although he mentions this report, Ganser (dis)qualifies it immediately by adding: 'But you have to remember that the NIST is a government department.' Again, the implication is clear: the authority simply couldn't be telling the truth.[20]

For Ganser, by contrast, the unresolved questions surrounding WTC 7 shake the edifice of lies constructed by the official explanation to its foundations. Although he again refrains from taking an overt position, his blunt statement, 'These are the critical seconds of 9/11 … Detonation or fire.

These are the only two possibilities', and the points he goes on to make after this dramatic utterance, speak volumes. He is at pains to mention, for example, that the CIA, the Secret Service and other governmental organizations were among the tenants of WTC 7. He claims explicitly that it was 'not just an ordinary building', the insinuation being that there was something to hide that somebody powerful wanted to get rid of. He also points out that the BBC reported the collapse too soon, thus employing the trope of foreknowledge so characteristic of conspiracist discourse.

The overall picture that emerges, therefore, is unambiguous: 9/11 was not an attack by Islamist terrorists that took the US government by surprise; nor was it an act of terrorism that government officials allowed to happen in order to derive political capital from it. Rather, the government itself was responsible for the attacks. Ganser never states this explicitly, but he doesn't need to. What he chooses to include and exclude, the way he handles particular subjects and arranges individual points into a coherent whole, the way he deploys all the strategies discussed earlier in this chapter – all this ultimately admits no other interpretation.[21]

Metaphors and more

A central characteristic of conspiracy theories already touched on in the previous chapter is the Manichean world view they embody. The conspiracy theorist believes himself to be on the trail of a conflict between absolute evil (the conspirators) and absolute good (their victims). In many texts, the alleged perpetrators are thus assigned exclusively negative character-istics, using metaphorically charged and at times apocalyptic language. For Cotton Mather, a Puritan minister who wrote an important report on the Salem witch trials of 1692, these events were quite literally the result of a Satanic conspiracy: 'An Army of Devils is horribly broke in upon this place', he writes, heavily influenced by the early modern notion that there was not just one, but many devils, who had now allied themselves with the witches and Native Americans against the Puritans. Some hundred years later, Augustin Barruel likens the founder of the Order of the Illuminati,

Adam Weishaupt, to the Devil in his *Memoirs Illustrating the History of Jacobinism*. In the 1830s, Samuel Morse describes the Catholic conspirators as being at least metaphorically in league with the Devil. 'The cloven foot has already shown itself', he writes of the first signs of the plot he claims to have uncovered. Shortly afterwards, he compares the conspirators' manoeuvres to those of a serpent. And during the 2016 US electoral campaign, Alex Jones claimed that Hillary Clinton and Barack Obama were demons from hell who attracted flies and smelt of sulphur.[22]

Another hallmark metaphor of conspiracist discourse is that of puppetry. It is used not only to expose the conspirators as the people secretly pulling the strings, but also to identify and criticize those supposedly used by them – willingly or otherwise – to achieve their ends. Conspiracy theories concerning Jews, Freemasons and Illuminati have used this imagery for centuries. In her essay about the European refugee crisis, the former news anchor Eva Herman brandishes the phrase 'Brussels puppet show', and there are countless videos on the internet claiming to prove that Barack Obama is a puppet of the New World Order.[23]

The metaphors for describing the progress of the conspiracy have also remained constant over the centuries. In the case of external conspiracies, the imagery usually comes from the military realm, presenting the plot in terms of an invasion. It is no coincidence that Cotton Mather speaks of an 'army' of devils assailing the Puritan community. Elsewhere, he likens the conspiracy of witches to an attack by 'vast regiments of French dragoons'. Similarly, Lyman Beecher, an influential Protestant minister who, like Samuel Morse, believed in the Catholic conspiracy against the USA, describes Catholic immigrants – believed to be entirely under the command of their priests – as 'an army of soldiers', while Morse fears that the enemy is already 'advancing beneath the very citadel'. Eva Herman also uses this kind of language, accusing the conspirators of misusing 'migrants as weapons' and repeatedly pointing out that most migrants arriving in Germany are 'strong, young men' who, moreover, do not come to the country with 'peaceful, help-seeking intent'.[24]

When it comes to internal plots conspiracy theorists frequently adopt the imagery of infection. To them, the concept of contagion makes it easier to understand how formerly exemplary citizens come to turn against their own community, sometimes making common cause with external enemies. There are two key moments in American history when conspiracy theorists proclaimed such a collaboration: the Salem witch trials and the Red Scare of the 1950s. In both cases, the conspiracist texts use the same metaphor. Thus, Cotton Mather describes witchcraft as a 'plague' and a 'poison ... that can't be cured' except by the power of God, whom he duly calls on to 'heal' the community. And soon after the Second World War, the American congressman George Dondero asserted that 'A few of [the communists] are aliens, but all of them are carriers of the same disease – the disease of Marxism.' J. Edgar Hoover, the head of the FBI, claimed that the 'infected' would turn into 'fanatics'. Louis Budenz, the communist turned anti-communist, recommended McCarthyism, that is, relentless anticommunism, as an antidote. The same kind of imagery was used by Johann August von Starck some 150 years earlier, when he accused the Freemasons of 'contaminating' society. Augustin Barruel, too, likened the crimes of the Illuminati to the 'ravages of the plague'.[25]

In the eyes of conspiracy theorists, the masses are in acute danger of infection because they are powerless and/ or completely unaware of the devious plot. Depending on the emphasis of the text, human beings are portrayed either as slaves or else as blind or asleep. The former approach highlights the fact that even perfectly normal people are being instrumentalized by the conspiracy. In his 'exposure' of a Catholic plot against the USA, Samuel Morse repeatedly describes the subjects of European rulers as slaves, and warns that such a fate will befall Americans too if nothing is done about the plot. The opposition he sets up between freedom and slavery forms the basis of many conspiracist texts, particularly in the USA. In an interview with Donald Trump in autumn 2015, for example, Alex Jones turns directly to the audience and asks: 'You wanna be free, or you wanna be slaves?'[26]

The dominant conspiracist strategy for suggesting the ignorance of the masses is to portray them as sleeping. They are said to go around with their eyes closed, unaware of what is happening under their noses. 'We may be asleep but the enemy is awake', writes Morse. If the enemy is alert and active, however, so are the conspiracy theorists. They have overcome their state of ignorance and are now attempting to 'awaken' other people and galvanize them into resisting the conspiracy. 'It is time to awake out of sleep', Lyman Beecher declares in his sermon, and Eva Herman exhorts her readers: 'Open your eyes!'[27] That said, many conspiracy theorists nowadays no longer believe that the majority of people even want to understand the truth. To them, therefore, those who label the discoverers of the plot 'conspiracy theorists' and dismiss their findings as absurd are either 'sheeple' themselves, as the terminology goes, or part of the conspiracy. Either way, this rhetoric constructs a stark contrast between the common herd and the few brave souls who seek to educate others, only to be treated with hostility.

One meme spread by a user on Pinterest puts the conspiracist's world view in a nutshell. According to this, 1 per cent of people are part of the conspiracy, 4 per cent are their puppets, and 90 per cent are 'asleep' and oblivious to what is going on around them. The remaining 5 per cent are those who claim to have discovered the truth and are attempting to alert the sleeping masses, something the 1 per cent naturally want to prevent. According to conspiracy theorists, they do this by stigmatizing conspiracist knowledge, which allows them to dismiss the revelations as nonsense. And conspiracy theorists generally agree that the conspirators will even resort to violence in order to suppress such information. Some conspiracy theories claim that John F. Kennedy was murdered because he wanted to bring the existence of extra-terrestrials to public attention. Another example is the alleged suicide of the journalist Danny Casolaro, who was found dead in his hotel room in Martinsburg, West Virginia in 1991. His family, along with many conspiracy theorists, do not believe that he took his own life, but suspect that he was murdered because he had uncovered a major conspiracy said to have helped Ronald Reagan to electoral victory in 1980.[28]

To the sceptical observer, this may raise the question of why, if they are so powerful and unscrupulous, the conspirators don't just do away with anyone who knows of their plans and reveals them to the public. In a TV programme broadcast by the BBC a few years ago, the *Times* journalist David Aaronovitch used this very argument to refute Alex Jones's New World Order conspiracy theories. 'How are you still alive?', he asked Jones, a fellow guest in the studio, thereby prompting a diatribe on the countless death threats Jones and his family have allegedly received. The presenter's dry objection, 'If they were going to kill you, they wouldn't threaten you', remained unanswered.[29]

This episode highlights the ambivalent image of the conspirator typically entertained by conspiracy theorists. On the one hand – as the above example shows – they are imagined as cruel and ruthless, yet on the other they are not able (or not bold enough) to get rid of people like Alex Jones. This is by no means the only inconsistency we encounter. Conspiracist texts nearly always present the conspirators as 'immoral supermen' whose supreme power is evident above all from their ability to control major historical processes over a period of years, decades or even centuries, and to manipulate the masses accordingly. At the same time, however, they are astonishingly incompetent. They leave clues everywhere, allowing the conspiracy theorists, once their eyes have been opened, to accumulate a wealth of evidence.[30]

Closely allied to this idea is the notion that conspirators are at once superhuman – because they are capable of casting aside their personal desires and vanities for years at a time in order to devote themselves to the conspiracy – and all too human, being driven by complexes and insecurities. In an extensive study conducted at the height of the Red Scare in the USA, for example, communists were described by L. Morris Ernst and David Loth as 'damaged souls'. According to them, it was individual psychopathological problems that determined whether a person became a good citizen or a communist conspirator. This was a neat conclusion because it not only removed the obligation to address the ideas behind communism, but also made it easier to identify the conspirators. In the anti-communist discourse of the time, anyone who did not fit the mainstream image, was homosexual or lived out of wedlock was readily suspected of being at least potentially an agent in the service of Moscow.[31]

It is no coincidence that conspiracy theorists often impute rampant or 'abnormal' sexuality to the alleged conspirators, or interpret such behaviour as signs of subversion. Commentators since Richard Hofstadter have identified this as a case of transference in the classical Freudian sense: the conspiracy theorists ascribe to the conspirators what they fail to recognize – or face up to – in themselves. That way it becomes not only possible, but indeed necessary, to focus on such topics in order to expose and then foil the conspiracy. If 'anti-Cathol-icism has always been the pornography of the Puritan', as Hofstadter pointedly puts it, then anti-Semitism and conspiracy theories about Illuminati, communists and the New World Order have served much the same purpose for their followers.[32] At the same time, projecting these charac-teristics onto the alleged conspirators enables the conspiracy theorist to construct a positive and largely consistent self-image. This is one of the many functions of conspiracy theories examined in the next chapter.

3

'Everything is connected', or: Why do people believe in conspiracy theories?

To Richard Hofstadter, the answer to this question was clear. In his 1964 essay 'The Paranoid Style in American Politics', he suggested that believers of conspiracy theories were suffering from mental health problems. Although he insists at the beginning of his text that the paranoia he ascribes to them should not be confused with the clinical variety described by Freud, he repeatedly makes this connection himself. His (incorrect) observation that, in the USA at least, only a minority of people have ever believed in conspiracy theories follows more or less logically from this pathologization: if conspiracy theorists have a different psychological disposition from that of 'normal' people, they must necessarily be in the minority, otherwise one could not call such belief a deviation from the norm.

Hofstadter's ideas, as already touched on in the introduction, exerted a lasting influence on research into conspiracy theories, and even today we still find occasional psychological studies deploying similar arguments and dismissing conspiracy theorists as mentally ill. In general, however, scholars across the disciplines agree by now that conspiracy theories are a mass phenomenon which requires a different approach. Many quantitative studies and opinion polls have found that conspiracy theories are far too widespread to be cast as an aberration. Moreover, cultural historians have shown that such theories were actually even more popular in the past, when they were still considered orthodox. Accordingly, history and cultural studies offer a very different answer to the question of why our ancestors believed in conspiracy theories from that of Hofstadter. While he held it to be a mark of abnormality, they regard it rather as one of normality.[1]

Why it was normal to be a conspiracy theorist, and why this changed over the course of the twentieth century, are questions I explore in the next chapter. In this chapter, I begin by looking at why, in an age when conspiracy theories are stigmatized and their followers frequently derided, so many people continue to believe in them. What are the benefits of conspiracy theories for individuals and groups? As I will show, they often fulfil the same functions as in the past, when they still passed for legitimate knowledge: conspiracy theories create meaning, reduce complexity and uncertainty, and emphasize human agency; they allow the supposed culprits to be identified and offer the hope that their activities can be stopped. In addition, they allow the conspiracy theorist to feel a sense of superiority over the unsuspecting masses. This aspect has been reinforced by the process of stigmatization, in that conspiracy theorists can now consciously position themselves in opposition to the mainstream and generally accepted beliefs of their society. In the second part of this chapter, I consider the question of which demographic groups are particularly 'susceptible' to conspiracy theories. However, my remarks on this subject are confined to the present and to the Western world – that is, to the time and place where conspiracy theories have undergone a process of delegitimization since the Second World War. Interestingly, quantitative disciplines such as psychology and qualitative ones such as cultural studies come to very different conclusions on this point. Next, I discuss the fact that some people circulate conspiracy theories out of political expediency or economic interest without necessarily believing them. The chapter concludes with a case study of Alex Jones, the most famous and financially successful American conspiracy theorist.

Functions

In *McCarthyism: The Fight for America*, a political pamphlet published in the election year 1952, Senator Joseph McCarthy, one of the most notorious conspiracy theorists of the twentieth century, begins by describing how he came to be convinced that the communist conspiracy was already controlling large parts of the American executive:

> Before meeting Jim Forrestal [at that time United States Secretary of the Navy] I thought we were losing to international Communism because of incompetence and stupidity on the part of our planners. I mentioned that to Forrestal. I shall never forget his answer. He said, 'McCarthy, consistency has never been the mark of stupidity. If they were merely stupid they would occasionally make a mistake in our favour.' This phrase struck me so forcefully that I have often used it since.[2]

The episode described here aptly illustrates the primary function of conspiracy theories, from which virtually all others follow. Conspiracy theories have always offered a particular way of explaining and making sense of the world. Where others see chaos or stupidity, they detect patterns and intentions. A large part of their attraction is their ability to connect disparate things, rejecting coincidence and contingency in favour of coherence and sinister intent. According to psychological studies, this is because conspiracy theories satisfy two universal human needs.

Firstly, evolution has trained the human brain to make connections and recognize patterns. This tendency, which drives not only conspiracism, but also other psychological phenomena such as prejudice, developed because it guaranteed the survival of the species. If someone died shortly after being bitten by a spider, the ability to connect these two events and, consequently, to avoid that species of spider in future could mean the difference between life and death for the rest of the group. Secondly, conspiracy theories offer a very specific explanation for the events in question. They do not argue, as the modern social sciences would do, that certain events are the result of systemic effects or structural constraints, or that a number of people behave in a seemingly coordinated way because they have similar interests or have been similarly socialized, i.e. they share the same habitus. Instead, conspiracy theories maintain that these events have been deliberately caused by a group of individuals. The need to understand events as the result of intentional actions is, as various experiments have consistently shown, another aspect of our genetic make-up.[3]

When conspiracy theorists claim that everything is connected, that there is no such thing as chance and that everything that happens was planned that way by somebody, they are giving expression to a deeply human tendency that makes evolutionary sense, but is at the same time misleading. As Rob Brotherton dryly puts it, 'The pattern-detection software built into our brain is exquisitely sensitive, but there's no built-in quality-control program to keep it in check.'[4] Our brains are inclined to see connections even where there are none, for example when two phenomena occur simultaneously or in quick succession by genuine coincidence. They are also wont to perceive intent where none exists. This is particularly evident in situations where no human actors are even involved, and we become infuriated with inanimate objects instead because it feels like they are 'conspiring' against us. Who hasn't had one of those mornings when the coffee machine overflows and then the front door jams, and we feel that life in general has it in for us? Although not everyone reacts like this when it comes to political events, there are some who do. For them, the idea that a group of malevolent conspirators are controlling our destiny is easier to accept than chaos and coincidence.

It should come as no surprise, then, that conspiracy theories also thrive in situations of uncertainty, or, to be more exact, among people who have trouble accepting uncertainty. Conspiracy theories resolve the ambiguity of complicated situations by providing a coherent account of what is going on and who is good and who is bad. And by translating the vague fear that people may be experiencing in such situations into a concrete one by grounding it in an alleged plot, they also equip people to deal better with this fear – because now they know what is happening and who is to blame.[5]

In other words, conspiracy theories – as already mentioned in Chapter 1 – hold fast to a very traditional image of humanity. By crediting human beings with the ability not only to know their own intentions, but to put them into practice, they understand them as autonomous individuals rather than subjects in the modern social scientific sense, which emphasizes the material and ideological constraints that govern people and determine their subjectivity. As such, contemporary conspiracy theories – in contrast to those of the eighteenth century, as we will see in the next chapter – are no longer in tune with the scientific thinking of the day. In the age of globalization and internet technology, however, when many processes appear increasingly beyond our control, their insistence on human agency is bound to remain attractive.

Even in the past, though, conspiracy theories served to uphold an increasingly obsolete view of humanity. A striking example of this is the debate around brainwashing that dominated American culture during the Red Scare of the 1950s. At that time, reputable social scientists seriously discussed whether American POWs in Korea might be brain-washed by the communist enemy into becoming 'sleeper agents'. This fear, which found its most potent cultural expression in John Frankenheimer's film *The Manchurian Candidate* (1962), was partly inspired by concerns that the modern consumer society had weakened Americans to such an extent that – unlike previous generations – they were no longer able to resist such attempts at manipulation. At the same time, however, as Timothy Melley has shown, the brainwashing debate also made it possible to talk about social conditioning without having to abandon the idea of the autonomous individual. While the victim was naturally no longer autonomous, their conditioning was not the result of indeterminate environmental influences, but was caused instead by the intentional actions of another individual, namely the brainwasher.[6]

By blaming events and developments that are perceived as pernicious and threatening on a group of consciously acting individuals rather than on abstract processes, conspiracy theories allow the identification of culprits. In contrast to the scapegoat theory of the anthropologist René Girard, where it is generally a single individual who is cast out of the community, conspiracy theories always focus by definition on several people, in what could be described as a collective form of 'othering'.[7] While some conspiracy theories remain extremely vague with regard to the perpetrators, others home in on the alleged leaders of the plot. In the case of Augustin Barruel, that person is Adam Weishaupt, the founder of the Order of the Illuminati; in that of Samuel Morse, it is Prince Metternich; in many 'Great Replacement' conspiracy theories, it is the Jewish–American billionaire George Soros, and in the currently thriving conspiracy theories about the coronavirus it is often Bill Gates.

As these examples show, conspiracy theories do not necessarily seek to banish a scapegoat from the community; often, the accusations are directed at actors who were never part of it in the first place. Nor is the use of violence against the alleged conspirators an inevitable consequence, either because they cannot be caught, or because the matter never goes beyond the revelation of their 'machinations'. Furthermore, the identification of the conspirators does not necessarily – as in the classical scapegoat theory – lead to the stabilization of a community in crisis. This function may be fulfilled when the conspiracy theory concentrates on 'external' enemies – something I discuss below using the example of the Iranian President Mahmoud Ahmadinejad, who repeatedly accused Israel and the USA of conspiracy. It is different, however, in the case of 'internal' enemies alleged to be undermining society, such as Freemasons or communists. Here, the objective of the conspiracy theorists is still to purge the traitors from the community, but since these traitors are imagined as extremely powerful and secretive, even those leading the charge seldom expect to be able to catch them all. By sowing mistrust among the members of a community, such conspiracy theories often have a destabilizing effect on its cohesion.

In addition, the practice of identifying specific culprits lends an almost utopian dimension to conspiracy theories. This may at first sound surprising, given that conspiracist narratives are about positively omnipotent enemies whose plots are invariably well advanced. Since the developments feared by conspiracy theorists are caused by human beings, however, they can also be stopped by human beings. Anyone who recognizes that the causes of migration, the effects of which are currently the subject of such intense debate all over the world, are highly complex, will not believe it possible to reverse this trend in the foreseeable future. Likewise, anyone who views the proliferation of alternatives to heterosexual partnership as a complex, gradual transformation of our society prompted by a wide variety of factors understands that this change is unstoppable. By contrast, anyone who sees migration flows as part of a conspiracy by a small group of bankers who are simultaneously driving the transformation of sexual and gender norms in order to weaken the Western nations will have a different attitude. To them, there is every possibility of stopping and reversing these damaging changes. It is 'simply' a matter of exposing and defeating the conspiracy – a perfectly conceivable prospect given the conspiracy theorist's insistence on human agency. In conspiracy theories, therefore, it is nearly always 'five minutes to midnight', but never 'just after midnight'. There is always still just enough time to stop the conspiracy.

This optimistic dimension of conspiracy theories comes to the fore more prominently than in most other cases in the so-called QAnon conspiracy theory, which emerged in October 2017 on 4chan. This theory holds that 'there is a worldwide cabal of Satan-worshiping pedophiles who rule the world, essentially, and they control everything. They control politicians, and they control the media. They control Hollywood, and they cover up their existence, essentially. And they would have continued ruling the world, were it not for the election of President Donald Trump.' Q, who might be one or more persons, does not provide evidence for the conspiracy of this evil elite, but delivers cryptic hints about how Trump and his allies are fighting this plot and what measures they are planning. Strictly speaking, then, this is not a new conspiracy theory but a twist on a number of already existing ones, especially long-standing accusations of satanism against liberal elites that were also used to smear Hillary Clinton during the 2016 election campaign. The interpretive work of identifying and exposing the plot is transformed here into the game of figuring out how the 'good guys' are foiling it. I say 'game' because the pressure to get it right is much lower than is usually the case in conspiracy theories. It is not about exposing the plot, but about understanding how it is being stopped.[8]

Just as conspiracy theories demonize the group of alleged conspirators, so they also idealize the group targeted by the conspiracy. The historian Dieter Groh calls this the 'unburdening or reducing function' of conspiracist thinking. To quote Groh's pithy phrase, conspiracy theories provide an explanation for why 'bad things happen to good people'.[9] Moreover, this emphasis on the victimhood of one's own group makes it appear not just superior to others (by virtue of its persecution by the conspirators), but good per se. This is another clear instance of the dualistic world view which, as we saw in Chapter 1, is typical of conspiracy theories. The fact that the group in question is being attacked by conspirators is a sign of its moral integrity. This is where the phenomenon of transference discussed at the end of the previous chapter comes in: the conspiracy theorists project onto the conspirators characteristics which they refuse to recognize in themselves.

This is not the only way in which the assumption of victimhood can have an unburdening effect, however: it also allows conspiracy theorists to put a positive spin on their own problematic characteristics. If someone rejected Barack Obama as president because he was black, and was bent on preventing Hillary Clinton from succeeding him because she was a woman, they exposed themselves, quite rightly, to accusations of racism and sexism. If they saw Obama and Clinton as puppets of the New World Order, on the other hand, they could shrug off such criticisms, at least in their own mind. The same goes for German conspiracy theories that stoke resentment against refugees. If migrants are not coming to Germany out of dire necessity, but as part of an insidious plan, resistance to their presence is not an expression of prejudice but a perfectly justifiable response.

It is also clear from the functions described so far that conspiracy theories by no means always have a socially isolating effect on their followers, or tend to attract people who have little contact with others. When such theories were regarded as legitimate knowledge, this situation would not have arisen in any case, as conspiracy theorists were only doing what the social norms demanded. Since the stigmatization of conspiracy theories, however, friendships and relationships are of course much more likely to suffer if only one party believes in them. At the same time, such beliefs can also be a passport to new social contacts – especially in the internet age, when followers of conspiracy theories only have to go online to find the affirmation that may be denied them in the real world. Through discussion forums, Facebook groups and YouTube channels, they can become part of a virtual community that serves as a substitute for the real one.

Lastly, it goes without saying that conspiracy theories fulfil important functions for those who produce and actively disseminate them. For one thing, belief in the existence of the plot gives them the necessary confirmation of their own special status. They stand apart from the common herd because – to use the conspiracist metaphor – they are no longer 'asleep', but have 'woken up' to what is really happening. Unlike the vast majority, they are no longer merely victims, but actors. In particular, the conspiracy theory allows suppliers of ever new 'revelations' to present themselves as the cognoscenti, bravely battling the conspiracy through persistent awareness raising. Some of them – like Alex Jones or David Icke – go on to achieve a high profile within the conspiracist community, accumulating considerable cultural and economic capital in the process.

This self-portrayal as the 'avant-garde' in the fight against conspiratorial activity, as Hofstadter put it, has always been important.[10] In the context of the stigmatization of conspiracy theories that has occurred over the last few decades, however, it has taken on a special significance. In the current situation, asserting the existence of a plot allows the conspiracy theorist to actively position themselves against the mainstream and its beliefs. In this way, those who commonly find themselves, or perceive themselves to be, marginalized, can turn their position of weakness into one of strength, and their imposed identity into a voluntary one. Their courageous efforts to spread the truth – even at the cost of being ridiculed or demonized by the majority of society and having to put up with real disadvantages – become an important part of their self-image. And they receive recognition from the community of those who share their belief in the existence of the conspiracy.

The important functions that conspiracy theories perform in terms of the individual and collective identity of those who believe in them explain why they generally remain unconvinced by counter-evidence, however conclusive it may be – in fact they may even reframe it as evidence of the plot. Anyone who questions the existence of the conspiracy is ultimately challenging the self-image of the conspiracy theorist and their membership of the group. It is normal for people to react negatively and even irrationally to such an assault on their identity, which is why it is not enough to confront conspiracy theorists with the 'facts' – a point I pursue at greater length in the conclusion.

Are conspiracy theories for losers?

According to the stereotype, the conspiracy theorist is a single, sexually frustrated middle-aged man. He has little in the way of a career and is perhaps even unemployed, with no friends and not much of a social life. He spends most of his days, and especially his nights, holed up in a small room in front of a computer (he may still be living with his parents), searching online for ever more evidence of some global conspiracy he uncovered a long time ago. In the real world, people react to his ideas with disbelief at best, and at worst with scorn and derision, resulting in his increasing isolation. His only source of affirmation is online, where he encounters likeminded people with whom he actively engages. Here, he is not a loser, but a member of a small, elite group who have understood what is really going on. His belief in conspiracy theories and membership of a virtual community allow him to feel superior to the masses. In reality, however, they are driving him further and further to the margins of society.

How far this cliché holds true is a question that is answered differently by different disciplines. Psychologists and political scientists, who have been studying conspiracy theories intensively for some years using quantitative methods such as questionnaires, would say: 'Not very'. Those working in qualitative disciplines, on the other hand, such as literary and cultural studies or anthropology, would contend that this image, although naturally exaggerated, does contain a grain of truth. From my – albeit partial – perspective, psychology and political science do provide important clues as to the types of people who believe in conspiracy theories, but the results require further elaboration in various respects, and indeed a degree of correction. In the following, therefore, I first examine the results of quantitative research and then discuss the perspective of cultural studies.

The overwhelming majority of psychological and political science research has concluded that gender, age and socio-economic status have little or no influence on belief in conspiracy theories. While some studies find that men are more likely to believe in them, others come to the exact opposite result, and most find no difference. As far as the impact of education on conspiracism goes, the studies present a mixed picture. Some conclude that the tendency towards conspiracism decreases with increasing levels of education, while others see no correlation between the two.[11]

By contrast, a whole series of studies have shown membership of an ethnic minority to be a substantial influencing factor. As long ago as 1994, in one of the first psychological investigations into this subject, Ted Goertzel concluded that African Americans and Americans with Hispanic roots were more inclined towards conspiracist explanations than white Americans. He attributes this to the historical experience of slavery and oppression, and society's failure to achieve equality in so many aspects of everyday life. According to Goertzel, awareness of actual conspiracies also plays a role, as demonstrated by frequent allusions to the Tuskegee syphilis study, in which US Public Health Service doctors infected black men with syphilis and left them untreated over a period of forty years in order to study the course of the disease.[12]

Goertzel's findings were confirmed in subsequent years by other studies which went on to emphasize the aspect of powerlessness more generally. Individuals and demographic groups who are excluded from political decision-making processes are more likely than others to regard them as being controlled by conspirators, leading the political scientists Joseph Uscinski and Joseph Parent to coin the memorable phrase 'conspiracy theories are for losers'.[13]

Another slew of studies insist that extreme political views are a highly reliable basis for predicting the existence of a 'conspiracy mentality' in a given individual. According to these studies, people located on the fringes of the political spectrum show a much stronger inclination towards conspiracist explanations than those with more moderate views. And this is the same for either end of the spectrum: the tendency towards conspiracy theories is almost as pronounced on the extreme left as it is on the extreme right, resulting in a classic U-shaped graph.[14]

Finally, a further group of studies attempts to correlate conspiracist beliefs with certain personality types. This is usually based on the five-factor model, whose components are openness to experience, conscientiousness, extraversion (i.e. sociability), agreeableness and neuroticism. Several studies have concluded that a correlation exists between openness to new experiences and belief in conspiracy theories. The researchers attribute this result to the fact that people who tend towards conspiracism are more receptive to explanations that run counter to the dominant beliefs of their society. As such, they are also more likely to believe in paranormal activities or UFOs, sharing as they do a preference for heterodox knowledge and alternative beliefs that are rejected by the mainstream.[15]

From a cultural studies perspective, there are two problems with the quantitative research on conspiracy theories. Firstly, it is only concerned with the present, which limits the frame of reference. This focus is of course rooted in the methodology. It is simply not possible to interview subjects from earlier centuries or obtain accurate responses from older subjects regarding their beliefs of a few decades ago. Since psychology assumes a continuity of mental processes over the course of history, however, the quantitative studies claim – at least implicitly – to explain conspiracist thinking of the past as well as the present. But the above-mentioned correlation between openness to explanations that deviate from the prevailing view only makes sense in the present climate, where conspiracy theories are stigmatized as counter-knowledge. It cannot apply to earlier times, when such knowledge was still legitimate (or indeed to non-Western cultures where this is still the case); if anything, the opposite would be true in these instances.

More problematic, however, is the fact that the quantitative studies are in many ways too imprecise – again as a

result of their methodology. Most studies present their interviewees with a series of statements and ask them to respond
to them on a scale normally ranging from 'strongly agree' to
'strongly disagree', with intermediate options such as 'mostly
agree', 'don't know' and 'mostly disagree'. What cannot be
measured in this way, however, is whether a given interviewee
'mostly agrees' with the statement 'The US government is
responsible for the September 11 attacks' because they have
already pondered it for some time and think it likely but are
not quite sure, or because they have never really thought
about the question and don't wish to appear naive, or indeed
because they consider US foreign policy to have created a
breeding ground for Islamist terrorism and hence for the
attacks. With this methodology, such important distinctions
are lost, and some people may consequently be categorized as
conspiracy theorists when, from another perspective, they are
nothing of the sort. Furthermore, the questionnaire method
provides no clues as to how important a given belief is to the
respondent's identity – in other words, what effect it has on
the way they live their lives. Quantitative studies, as many
of the scholars who conduct them readily admit, measure
belief in conspiracy theories, but they do not really study
conspiracy theorists, that is, people for whom belief in one
or more conspiracy theories is a central part of who they are.

This helps to explain the diverging evaluations of the
gender factor. While quantitative disciplines regard conspiracism as gender-neutral, most qualitative disciplines take the
exact opposite view. Now as in the past, the conspiracist
texts, images and videos studied by cultural studies scholars
are produced almost exclusively by men. The same goes for
the majority of comments left under videos, blog entries or
articles with conspiracist content. Granted, it is and always
has been much easier for men in the patriarchally structured
societies of the Western world to present their conspiracist
ideas to the public and gain a hearing. And there are of course
examples of significant female conspiracy theorists both past
and present, such as Nesta Webster who, at the beginning of
the twentieth century, was the first person to systematically
associate the Illuminati with communism. Nevertheless, it is
men who invest most time and effort in spreading, consuming
and commenting on conspiracy theories. Another reason for

this, which I will turn to in a moment, is that conspiracy theories are – at least at the present time – much more important to the male than to the female identity.

That said, as Annika Thiem points out, 'there is hardly any ethnographic research and thus almost no empirical data to either confirm or refute the claim that conspiracy theorists are more likely to be men than women. Fieldwork studies of conspiracy theorists and their communities are rare and often do not live up to academic and ethical standards.'[16] This is partly because conspiracy theorists often feel that they are not taken seriously by academics and therefore decline to participate. As a consequence, it tends to be journalists who research these milieus – undercover and without seeking the consent the ethics of ethnography demands.

Another reason, however, is that disciplines involving fieldwork are only just beginning to address this issue. If more work is done on this in future, the findings on gender will doubtless be refined. The research conducted by Jaron Harambam, who studied the Dutch conspiracist community over several years, certainly indicates that the type of conspiracy theory also has a bearing on whether it is more likely to be believed by women or by men. According to Harambam, Dutch men lean more towards large-scale political conspiracy theories such as 9/11 and the New World Order, and women towards those with a more direct impact on their own lives, such as chemtrails or vaccines. Although men believe in these too of course, they tend to see them as pieces in a giant superconspiracy puzzle.[17]

From the perspective of cultural studies, it is quite plausible that education should have an impact on belief in conspiracy theories. That said, it presumably depends – and this explains why some psychological studies detect a correlation while others do not – not just upon a person's level of education, but on the precise content of what they have learned at school or university or through self-study. As we have seen, conspiracy theories perpetuate an antiquated image of humanity in their insistence on intentionalism and human agency. It is therefore highly probable that people whose education has familiarized them with nuanced ideas about how human beings tick and societies function – psychologists, sociologists or historians, for example – will be less attracted to conspiracy theories than people who have never seriously engaged with the standpoints of these disciplines.

The findings of quantitative research on the correlation between conspiracy theories and powerlessness are very important. In my view, however, they need to be modified to take into account the fact that it is not necessarily actual powerlessness that spawns such beliefs, but the feeling of being powerless, or the fear of becoming so. It is not the actual political influence of an individual or group that matters, nor their real socio-economic status, but how they perceive their own situation. This accounts for the spread of conspiracy theories among blacks and Latinos in the USA that has been observed in several psychological studies; conversely, it also helps explain why such ideas are common among supporters of the far-right Alternative for Germany, for example, whose economic status is often not exactly precarious.[18]

The most striking example of this is of course the populist movements that have garnered so much support in North America and Europe in recent years. These movements – on either side of the Atlantic – are carried not by those who have actually been left behind economically or otherwise, but rather by those who fear such marginalization and wish to avoid it: people who, in an age of globalization, are worried about their jobs or their pensions, and who see themselves and their country as threatened by changing moral values and increasing ethnic diversity. Within these demographic groups, conspiracy theories are rife for the reasons discussed above. They attribute developments which, although disparate, are perceived as similarly threatening, to a single explanation – namely a large-scale plot – and express the hope that these changes can be stopped and reversed if the conspiracy is exposed and defeated.[19]

It is no coincidence that these populist movements, in which conspiracy theories hold such sway, are overwhelmingly supported by men. Similarly, more men than women voted for Donald Trump; and in the case of Pegida, a social movement based in the East German city of Dresden that has been protesting for many years against the alleged Islamization of the West, up to 75 per cent of those who regularly join the protests are male. Men feel particularly threatened by the developments that are fuelling the current populist trend and the conspiracy theories so closely bound up with it – an issue I discuss in detail at the end of the next chapter. The male identity is associated much more markedly than the female one with the role of breadwinner, and hence with properly paid employment. It is not just on the economic front that men have more to lose than women, though. For a long time, white men in particular – even those on a low income – have ranked above women and non-whites in the social hierarchy. The advent of a black president and a female German chancellor, however, along with the perceived threat of losing their women to non-white migrants – whether Mexicans in the USA or North African refugees in Germany – has fuelled anxieties within this group. And conspiracy theories are a way of articulating those anxieties.[20]

The few studies conducted to date on the sociodemographic make-up of the Pegida marches in Dresden also show the average age of the demonstrators to be around forty-seven.[21] This, too, is unsurprising, given that the factors driving both populism and conspiracism are particularly relevant to this age group. These are people who are some way off retirement, and hence directly affected by the transformations they attribute to a conspiracy, yet old enough to be nostalgic for a supposedly better past, the last vestiges of which are threatening to disappear before their eyes. The psychological studies outlined above are surely right to conclude that conspiracism per se is not confined to either the left or the right of the political spectrum – categories which are in any case being radically challenged by populism. But conspiracy theories are always ultimately conservative in the sense that they seek to maintain or restore a threatened order.

In short, the image of the conspiracy theorist outlined at the beginning of this section and encountered so often in popular culture is a vast exaggeration. Belief in conspiracy theories is not restricted to any gender, age, ethnicity or income bracket. Education only reduces our susceptibility to conspiracy theories if we have learnt the 'right' things. It is, however, fair to say that – in contemporary Western societies at least – those most susceptible to such ideas tend to be men who already feel marginalized or are afraid of slipping down the social ladder. In other words, conspiracy theories are not – to quote the political scientists Uscinski and Parent – 'for losers', but for those who are afraid of becoming losers, or already identify as such.

Propaganda and commerce

Up to now I have – both in this chapter and in the book as a whole – tacitly assumed that those who spread conspiracy theories do so from a desire to bring the truth to light. While this is indeed mostly the case, there are plenty of other reasons for voicing conspiracy theories. Some do it for political motives, in order to provoke a certain reaction among their supporters, for example, while others are driven by commercial interests. Although neither case precludes a belief in the truth of one's own accusations, it is not a prerequisite. It is quite probable that Senator Joe McCarthy, the most high-profile figure in the communist witch-hunt of the 1950s, genuinely believed in the existence of a Moscow-led conspiracy. But that didn't prevent him from using his suspicions to great strategic effect over a long period of time. By contrast, Donald Trump – as I discuss in more detail in the next chapter – is unlikely to have believed in most of the conspiracy theories he spread during the election campaign. As outsiders, we cannot of course claim either of these things with absolute certainty, since we, like the conspiracy theorists themselves, have to rely on circumstantial evidence and deduction. Proving them is like trying to establish a writer's intention – something that literary scholars wisely no longer attempt. What is clear, however, is that conspiracy theories are routinely used in order to accumulate political or other kinds of capital. And it is also clear that – whatever the beliefs of their authors – this strategy only works if there is an audience willing to believe the allegations.

One politician notable for his consistent use of conspiracy theories is Mahmoud Ahmadinejad, president of Iran from 2005 to 2013. Throughout his presidency, he regularly made waves with his conspiracist allegations against Western powers, notably the USA and Israel. He repeatedly denied the Holocaust, for example, describing it as a Zionist invention intended to legitimize the existence of the state of Israel. In September 2012, when Iran was suffering the effects of a drought, he accused the West of deliberately causing the disaster, claiming that Western scientists were destroying the rain clouds before they reached Iran in order to inflict harm on the country's population. Two years previously, in his speech to the UN General Assembly, he had accused the USA of carrying out the attacks of 11 September 2001 itself to create a pretext for the invasions of Afghanistan and Iraq. Although these and other accusations provoked indignation in New York and throughout the West, Ahmadinejad's target audience lay elsewhere. His conspiracy theories demonized the USA and Israel in order to deflect attention from or even defuse conflicts at home. By raising the spectre of an external conspiracy, he sought to forge a sense of national unity.[22]

A somewhat different example is that of the 'Lisa case', which hit the headlines in Germany and Russia in January 2016 and led to diplomatic tensions. It concerned a then thirteen-year-old Russian-German girl from Berlin, who failed to return home one evening and was reported missing by her parents. When she turned up again the next day, she initially said that she had been kidnapped and raped by three Arabic-speaking men, but quickly changed her story when questioned by police. Eventually, it turned out that she had spent the night with a boyfriend. The Russian media took up the case, however, claiming that the German government was covering up the fact that Lisa had been raped by refugees. Russian Germans in Berlin took to the streets, expressing fear for the safety of their children and calling on the government to take action. Even the Russian Foreign Minister, Sergey Lavrov, accused the German authorities of concealing what really happened.[23]

This was not an explicit allegation of conspiracy in the sense that it did not identify some master plan behind the cover-up, but it didn't need to do that in a climate where conspiracy theories surrounding migrants command considerable support. The Russian media coverage simply played on existing anxieties. And just as the example of Ahmadinejad shows how conspiracy theories can be instrumentalized in order to strengthen the cohesion of one's own country, so the Lisa case demonstrates how conspiracy allegations can be used to destabilize another country. According to the East StratCom Task Force, a unit of the EU External Action

Service dedicated to debunking disinformation deliberately spread by the pro-Kremlin media, the reporting in this case was an instance of 'kite-flying', enabling Russia to gauge how the German public and politicians would react.[24]

While it is not clear whether Ahmadinejad believed his own conspiracy theories or not, it is quite obvious in the Lisa case that the Russian media were consciously putting out a false story. This is an example of fake news, that is, disinformation deliberately circulated with the aim of discrediting certain individuals or institutions – in this case the German government and police – in order to achieve a particular objective. Fake news has attracted much attention recently, and the term is sometimes even used as a synonym for conspiracy theories. But not all conspiracy theories are fake news, and vice versa. Many conspiracy theorists are genuinely convinced that they have hit upon a plot; and not all deliberately circulated disinformation asserts the existence of a conspiracy.[25]

It is no coincidence that the examples I have chosen to illustrate the political instrumentalization of conspiracy theories do not come from the Western world. Since conspiracy theories have been relegated to the realm of stigmatized knowledge there for decades, politicians and mainstream media cannot draw as freely on this kind of rhetoric as their counterparts in large parts of the Islamic world or Russia. There are occasional exceptions to this rule, such as the claim by the Bush administration in the lead-up to the invasion of Iraq that Saddam Hussein was in league with Osama bin Laden, or the conspiracist rhetoric of Donald Trump, which I examine more closely in Chapter 5. Rather, the people actively spreading conspiracy theories in Europe and North America today are – as we saw in the last chapter – those who position themselves deliberately against the mainstream and official explanations of particular events. That is not to say that there is no audience for such counter-narratives. On the contrary, there are stars of the conspiracist scene on both sides of the Atlantic who have built up a considerable fan community and are thus able to earn a living from their conspiracy theories. This naturally affects the methods they use to promote their beliefs.

One example is David Icke, the professional footballer

and sports reporter turned British Green Party spokesman mentioned briefly in Chapter 1, who became a 'full-time' conspiracy theorist over twenty years ago. Icke has written a string of books exposing the plot of an elite group of extra-terrestrial reptiles who he believes are controlling the fate of the world; he also disseminates these theories around the globe via lectures lasting several hours (the current admission charge in the UK is around twenty-five pounds). He runs a professional website including an online store where you can buy his books and tickets to his lectures, alongside posters, T-shirts and other fan merchandise. And since Icke – like all conspiracy theorists who make a living from their ideas – faces the problem of having to incorporate new elements into his theories all the time in order to remain up to date and keep loyal fans supplied with fresh material, he posts a new video on the website every week in which he examines the events of the previous days for conspiracies, along with an option to subscribe to a monthly newsletter, and a discussion forum in which he also participates. None of this is free, by the way: as of 15 April 2019, it cost £5.39 for a single month or £3.70 per month for an annual subscription. In short, anyone wishing to share in David Icke's latest insights must invest not only time, but money as well.

Not that the economic pressure of having to keep up a constant commentary on current affairs presents any challenge to Icke's imagination. Not only is the idea that everything is connected a fundamental principle of conspiracism: what Icke is pushing is the most comprehensive superconspiracy theory currently in existence. From the alleged creation of human beings by extra-terrestrials as a slave race, through the ritual murders of the Middle Ages to the death of Princess Diana and the attacks of 9/11, everything has a place in his narrative. Thus, the Ukrainian crisis, the attack on the editors of *Charlie Hebdo*, migration flows and the Syrian conflict can be readily incorporated, along with anything else that may happen in the meantime.

Although the case of the Swiss conspiracy theorist Daniele Ganser is a rather different one, here too we can see how revelation techniques are influenced by economic interests. Whereas Icke actively appropriates the term conspiracy theory, mentioning proudly on his homepage that his book

The Biggest Secret 'has been called the conspiracy theorist's Rosetta Stone', Ganser rejects this label.[26] As we saw in Chapter 2, he uses a form of rhetoric that claims to simply ask questions and flag up contradictions. Moreover, the conspiracy theory that Ganser implicitly develops is much less comprehensive. While Icke's superconspiracy theory encompasses virtually every existing event and system conspiracy, Ganser 'restricts' himself to the US government, the CIA and NATO. Nevertheless, he too is driven by the need to keep up with the times. Since he, like Icke, earns a living from his books and lectures (tickets for the latter vary in price according to the promoter, but the average charge is around thirty francs or euros per person), he is under similar pressure to continue expanding his conspiracy theory.

Other than this, it is very hard to explain why Ganser has in recent years branched out into writing on the Ukrainian crisis, the Turkish coup or the Syrian conflict, and makes at least a brief digression into these events during his lectures on the USA and 9/11. In so doing he is, after all, undermining his own efforts to present himself as a serious historian, since – as he openly admits – he is unable to read Turkish and Arabic sources in the original, and has to rely on translations. This takes to new lengths the uncritical acceptance of his sources already criticized by reviewers of his dissertation. Unsurprisingly, Ganser takes the same characteristically indirect approach when presenting conspiracist ideas relating to Syria, Turkey or other current events. In a telephone interview with an alternative news magazine in January 2015, for example, he concentrates on the alleged contradictions and gaps in the official version of the attacks on the satirical magazine *Charlie Hebdo* in Paris a few days before, suggesting that it could also have been a 'false flag' operation by a Western intelligence service designed to inflame the conflict with the Islamic world. And in a lecture delivered in June 2017 on the failed Turkish coup of 2016, Ganser presents the CIA's alleged support of the earlier military coup of 1980 – for which there is no evidence apart from a few dubious anecdotes – as proven, in order to argue for the likelihood of further CIA involvement. In Ganser's world too, therefore – if not as explicitly as in Icke's – everything is ultimately connected, and, as with Icke, it all appears to be motivated less by conviction than by the necessity of staying in business.[27]

Case study: Alex Jones

David Icke and Daniele Ganser, however, are mere small fry by comparison with Alex Jones, the most famous and commercially successful conspiracy theorist in the USA, and probably in the entire world. Jones still works in Austin, the capital of Texas, where he was born in 1974. After graduating from high school, he briefly attended college but soon gave up his studies to pursue a career in the media. His conspiracist 'awakening' was probably Timothy McVeigh's 1995 bomb attack on a government building in Oklahoma City, in which 168 people lost their lives, including nineteen babies and small children. McVeigh, who was subsequently sentenced to death and executed in 2001, cited the conspiracy of the New World Order against the population of the United States as justification for his crime. But many other believers of this conspiracy theory have cast doubt on McVeigh's role in the bombing. One of these was Jones, who publicly accused the government of involvement in the attacks. Thereafter, he began to spread conspiracy theories increasingly via his show *The Final Edition* on the radio station KJFK. This did no harm to his popularity with listeners, but it upset the station's advertisers, resulting in Jones's dismissal from KJFK in 1999. He then went freelance, founded the website infowars.com and began producing his own programme, *The Alex Jones Show*, earning his living from conspiracy theories from then on.

While the 9/11 Truth Movement, which attracted many people with no obvious history as conspiracy theorists, only formed in the wake of the Iraq War in 2003, Jones claimed immediately after the attacks that the government was responsible for them and that he had seen them coming. It is true that Jones had repeatedly accused the government of planning a second Oklahoma City, but he had been no more specific than that. Consequently, he could easily incorporate the events of 9/11 into the narrative of the New World Order, in which Barack Obama – another alleged puppet of the NWO – also figured in subsequent years.[28]

Jones proved extremely adept at spreading his superconspiracy theory and exploiting its commercial potential. His radio show has mushroomed into a veritable media empire enabling him to reach millions of people. It is broadcast by over sixty US stations and can be streamed live on the internet. He also has an internet-based television channel, prisonplanet.tv. More than sixty people are employed in the production of content for the show and various platforms. And there is certainly no shortage of material: in terms of scope, Jones's theory of a superconspiracy involving international elites is – aliens aside – of a similar order to David Icke's. Everything that happens can be integrated somehow or other into the narrative.

The show is punctuated by several commercial breaks featuring video clips or personal interventions by Jones to promote his own range of products relating directly to his conspiracist ideas. From water purification tablets to tents, there is everything you would need to survive in the wilderness if the New World Order provoked a war and you were forced to flee in its wake. There are also products which can be used (allegedly) to neutralize the effects of the toxins that the conspirators (allegedly) put in our water and food supplies in order to keep us docile. Advertised remedies include 'Brain Force Plus' capsules to restore our ability to think for ourselves, and even 'Super Male Vitality', designed to counteract the feminizing effect of the toxins and ensure that there is no lack of energy in the fight for freedom. All this comes with a price tag, of course: a small bottle of 'Super Male Vitality' – equivalent to a month's supply – will set you back $59.95.

Despite his evident popularity among some sections of the American public and his considerable commercial success, Alex Jones was for a long time a marginal figure in the USA. He was mostly ignored, sometimes mocked and consistently censured by the mainstream, as when he claimed, for instance, that the December 2012 massacre at Sandy Hook Elementary School – an episode that claimed the lives of almost thirty people, most of them children – was staged by the government in order to restrict the right to bear arms that is sacrosanct to so many Americans. Following Donald Trump's announcement of his candidacy for president in summer 2015, however, Jones ceased to be ignored, and is now taken seriously. He threw himself instantly behind Trump and took every opportunity to support his election campaign.

One example of this was his endorsement of Trump's entirely fabricated claim that Arabs living in New Jersey had rejoiced over the collapse of the World Trade Center towers. When Trump appeared via Skype on Jones's show in December 2015, Jones began the interview with the words: 'You are vindicated, this is gotta be the fiftieth time the last six months, on the radical Muslims celebrating not just in New Jersey, but New York, Palestine, all over it. What do you have to say? They are still attacking you. ... What's going on here?'[29] Trump rewarded him for this engagement not just by appearing on his show, but by praising him repeatedly during the election campaign, inviting him in summer 2016 to the Republican National Convention in Cleveland, where Jones met with Trump's adviser Roger Stone, and in 2017 accrediting infowars.com for White House press conferences.

Perhaps this was why Jones continued to stand by Trump so assiduously when many of his most zealous election campaign supporters turned their back on him in late summer 2017, accusing the president of failing to keep his promises. Since then, however, the relationship between the two men has become somewhat tarnished, following an air strike on Syria ordered by Trump which Jones evidently saw as a betrayal of the president's nationalist agenda. In a YouTube livestream he declared, 'They have broken Trump', and complained that Trump had not called him 'in six months'. In an interview with Joe Rogan in February 2019, Jones again expressed his evident disappointment at Trump's failure to act consistently as he would wish: 'I don't dislike Donald Trump and I think he's done some good things, on trying to do peace and trying to get jobs back to America, but I hate Donald Trump because I got behind him ... and then he became my identity', he told the former comedian during a recording for his podcast, *The Joe Rogan Experience*.[30]

This highly cryptic statement may also have been motivated by Jones's eventual realization that the attention his closeness to Trump has brought him in recent years from anti-conspiracist elements of the public is not always an

advantage. In his show *Last Week Tonight*, for example, the
satirist John Oliver spent some time picking apart Jones's
conspiracy theories and in particular his business model. And
in February 2017, the German weekly *Der Spiegel* ran an
in-depth feature on Jones. 'Trump and I have talked several
times since the election. About freedom and our common
goal to destroy our enemies', Jones told the journalist in
the interview. Partly as a result of reports like this, Jones's
conspiracy theories have been taken far more seriously –
and sanctioned more severely – since Trump's election. In
summer 2018, for instance, Facebook, YouTube, Twitter and
a number of other platforms deleted all articles by Jones and
Infowars because their conspiracist and often inflammatory
content violated the terms of use. This was a blow for Jones,
whose YouTube channel had previously attracted more than
2.1. million subscribers, and who commanded a Facebook
following of over 1.5 million, but it posed no threat to his
business model, since all content from the Infowars site is
readily available either on the site itself or elsewhere on the
web. More problematic for him was PayPal's decision in
summer 2018 to stop processing transactions with his site.[31]

Despite actively defending his business interests, however,
Jones is also ready and able to deny his conspiracist beliefs
where necessary. Thus, he has publicly apologized on several
occasions in the past when individuals or institutions he
has accused of being part of some conspiracy or other have
brought pressure to bear on him through their lawyers. One
notable instance was his statement of March 2019 in response
to a lawsuit filed by the father of one of the children killed in
the 2012 shooting at Sandy Hook Elementary School. Jones
had repeatedly accused him and the families of the other
victims of being 'crisis actors' party to a government plot.
While Jones stopped short of an apology in his affidavit,
he acknowledged that the killing spree was indeed real and
explained his earlier claim by asserting that he had not
always been of sound mind:

> I, myself, have almost had like a form of psychosis back in
> the past where I basically thought everything was staged, even
> though I'm now learning a lot of times things aren't staged.
> So I think, as a pundit, someone giving an opinion, that, you

know, my opinions have been wrong; but they were never wrong consciously to hurt people.[32]

This explanation is rather neat because it allows Jones to reject the accusation that he deliberately lied, while simultaneously playing on the prejudices of the other parties. Essentially, Jones is echoing the idea – widespread since Richard Hofstadter's classic 1964 essay on 'The Paranoid Style in American Politics' – that conspiracy theorists are mentally ill. Clearly, this is a highly strategic move designed to avoid any negative consequences.

A similarly strategic approach was observable in Jones's dispute with his ex-wife Kelly over custody of their three children. The case was tried in court in April 2017 and ended in a victory for his ex-wife. Her solicitors' strategy was to paint Jones as an irresponsible conspiracy theorist who had lost his grip on reality. His emotional outbursts on camera, his spurious accusations and his trivialization of Donald Trump's sexist remarks showed that he was not fit to be entrusted with the care of children. For their part, Jones's solicitors argued that he was a 'performance artist'. He presented a satirical caricature on-screen that had nothing to do with his true personality and therefore had no impact on the fulfilment of his duties as a father. 'I don't want to think about work when I go home', Jones told the court – a statement strikingly at odds with his remark to the *Spiegel* reporter a few weeks before: 'It's hard to switch off. I constantly see propaganda everywhere.'[33] Finally, in a video published on infowars.com the evening after his statement, he appealed directly to his fans, claiming that he had in no way distanced himself in court from his comments in the show: 'They've got articles out today that say I'm fake, all of this other crap. Total bull. ... The media is deceiving everywhere. I 110-percent believe what I stand for.'[34]

This balancing act certainly doesn't seem to have done him any harm in the eyes of his fans, as his show remains as popular as ever. Anyone who believes the conspiracy theories expressed in *The Alex Jones Show* is probably convinced either that Jones was forced to deny his true beliefs in court for strategic reasons, or that he did no such thing, and was merely the victim of an attempt by the conspiracy-controlled mainstream media to discredit him. This is a prime example of the fragmentation of the public sphere – the endpoint of the historical development I discuss in the next two chapters.

4

The story so far, or: How have conspiracy theories evolved historically?

In the previous chapters, I have already noted that both the form and functions of conspiracy theories have changed over time – due partly to the emergence of new media, and partly to the shift in the status of such theories from legitimate to illegitimate knowledge. So far I have examined conspiracy theories systematically; in this chapter I focus on their historical development. I do not claim to give a comprehensive account of the transformation of conspiracist ideas from antiquity to the present. Quite apart from the fact that such an account could not be fitted into one chapter, it is in any case not currently possible, since we still know far too little about large parts of that history. A good deal of research has been done on the USA, but as far as Europe is concerned, the studies undertaken so far only relate to individual regions and periods, and do not yet add up to a coherent overall picture. And while some studies exist on the current spread of conspiracy theories in the Arab world, research into the historical development of conspiracism in this region, as well as in Asia, has not even begun.

Moreover, there is absolutely no guarantee that we would find conspiracy theories in the history of Asia or the Arab world. Contrary to the assumptions of early researchers, conspiracy theories – by the relatively narrow definition I use in this book – are not an anthropological constant.

This observation is not as surprising as it might seem at first sight, given that conspiracist suspicions, as I have shown in the previous chapters, require certain conditions that do not apply at all times and in all locations. Firstly, conspiracy theories are based on particular assumptions about human agency and hence on a particular understanding of the subject. And since they relate to plots that began in the past, are perceptible in the present and aspire to fulfilment in the future, they presuppose a specific understanding of temporality and historical development. Secondly, conspiracy theories require some kind of public sphere where they can be circulated orally, in written form, as images, or electronically. Thirdly, therefore, the emergence and evolution of conspiracy theories is always dependent upon certain media conditions. Conspiracy theories are complex narratives, although they can be reduced to the basics in everyday conversation. These basics can be spread in casual conversation, but what we are dealing with then are conspiracy rumours rather than genuine conspiracy theories.[1]

Until we can state with certainty that conspiracy theories already existed in Asia and the Islamic world before they came into contact with the West, we cannot disprove the hypothesis that conspiracy theories are an originally European concept which – after a brief flowering during antiquity – evolved between the early modern period and the Enlightenment, and was exported around the world in the wake of colonialism and imperialism. This may be an uncomfortably Eurocentric notion, but it's what current research suggests. If true, it would be reasonable to assume that European conspiracy theories came into contact with related indigenous concepts, such as specific forms of occultism, in Africa, Asia and the Americas, and that this resulted in hybridizations which in turn – since cultural transfer is never just a one-way street – influenced conspiracy theories in Europe. All this is still completely uncharted territory, however. All we know is that conspiracy theories exist today in a very similar form throughout the world.

In this chapter, therefore, my historical account is restricted to Europe and the USA. In the first section, I give a brief outline of the evolution of modern-style conspiracy theories, with the emphasis on Western and Central Europe. Both there and in the USA, conspiracy theories long constituted a perfectly legitimate form of knowledge firmly rooted in mainstream society and propagated by elites and ordinary people alike. My overview concludes with the Second World War, this being the point at which conspiracist thinking began to be delegitimized in the Western world. Since this development has so far only been studied with regard to the USA, the second section focuses on that country. But the process of marginalization is likely to have followed a very similar pattern in Europe. The third section is devoted to a case study of anti-Semitic conspiracy theories. These offer a classic illustration of the developments outlined in the previous sections, having been well researched due to their terrible consequences over the course of history. Furthermore, the sad fact of their lingering popularity makes it possible to analyse the changes brought about by the shifting status of conspiracy theories. In the last section I discuss the relationship between conspiracy theories and populism already mentioned at various points in this book.

Emergence and development up to the twentieth century

For Karl Popper, who coined the term 'conspiracy theory' in its modern sense, conspiracism is a product of the European Enlightenment, 'a typical result of the secularization of a religious superstition'. According to Popper, the decline of trust in the divine plan of salvation and creation created a void. Incapable of accepting a world of chaos and chance, and not yet familiar with the theories of the modern social sciences, people clung to the structure of the religious paradigm. The 'Homeric gods' of the past were now superseded by 'powerful men ... whose wickedness is responsible for all the evils we suffer from'.[2]

There is much to be said for this secularization theory. Conspiracy theories flourished in the age of the Enlightenment and, notably in the context of the French Revolution, authors such as Barruel and Starck developed explanatory models that were no different from the conspiracy theories of the present. Moreover, such theories, as noted in the

previous chapter, serve a range of functions – among them
the creation of meaning and identity – that used to be, and
indeed still are, fulfilled by religions. And just as the followers
of a religion refuse to accept evidence against its claims,
so committed conspiracy theorists can never be convinced
by conclusive counter-evidence. It is not for nothing that
adherents of conspiracy theories are referred to as believers.
Nevertheless, conspiracy theories did not replace religion
after the eighteenth century, nor are conspiracy theories and
religion mutually incompatible. As we shall see, there were
a number of pre-Enlightenment conspiracy scenarios that
saw the Antichrist or the Devil as the author of the plot,
and even today there is still a 'religious' version of almost
every popular conspiracy theory in which the Antichrist or
similar otherworldly agents are the masterminds. Indeed,
even the idea of the Homeric gods is not incompatible with
secularized conspiracy theories.[3]

As Joseph Roisman and Victoria Emma Pagán have shown,
there are numerous examples of conspiracist suspicions in
antiquity that differ only marginally from modern-day ones.
This is because the conditions outlined at the beginning of
this chapter applied likewise to ancient Athens and Rome.
Although both cultures ascribed more power to fate than
modern conspiracy theories do, Athenians and Romans
shared the same belief in the human ability to forge plans
and act upon them. What's more, there was a public arena
in which conspiracist ideas could circulate for maximum
impact. In marked contrast to today, however, this happened
not just in written form, but verbally too. Conspiracy
theories were not just a feature of everyday communication,
in the sense of unsubstantiated rumours reduced to mere
claims and assumptions, but an integral part of the elaborate
speeches before public gatherings or in court that epitomized
the political culture of Athens and Rome. These speeches
were often written down in advance and carefully copied by
scribes onto scrolls for subsequent publication, which is how
they have survived for posterity.[4]

As in modern times, the purpose of ancient conspiracy
theories was to rule out chaos and chance. Then as now,
the necessarily secret conspiracy had to be deduced from
observable reality and, just like today, conspiracy allegations

served to identify enemies, strengthen the identity of one's own group and distinguish the conspiracy theorist from the ignorant masses. Similarly, suspicions could focus on external or internal enemies, or often on a combination of both. In Lysias' speech *Against Agoratus*, for example, the unnamed and unknown prosecutor accuses representatives of a variety of groups in Athens – including the Council of the Five Hundred and the oligarchs – of involvement in the plot against the polis. Later, there were countless conspiracy theories surrounding Philip II of Macedon, who was alleged to have plotted the destruction of democracy together with traitors inside Athens. The urtext of Roman conspiracism, on the other hand, is Cicero's orations *Against Verres*, in which the author goes far beyond the verifiable allegations against the governor of the province of Sicily, accusing him, among other things, of supporting slave revolts that never actually took place. This he does via supposedly unequivocal witness statements and dubious deductions – a method that foreshadows those of modern conspiracy theorists.[5]

After this first flowering of conspiracism, however, it was some time before similar suspicions and arguments reared their heads again. Contrary to common claims, there were no medieval conspiracy theories in the narrower sense, since there was neither an audience for the accusations nor the understanding of temporality necessary for such theories. There were periodic outbreaks of suspicion against Jews and other groups, and to that extent we can recognize certain stock themes of conspiracism, but in the vast majority of cases the accuser's aim was to justify already perpetrated acts of violence by insinuating that the victims were involved in a plot, and not to expose an ongoing intrigue. The argumentation characteristic of conspiracy theories, which I discussed in Chapter 2, is entirely absent, and does not resurface – together with more typical conspiracy scenarios – until the early modern period, when the invention of the printing press contributed to the emergence of conspiracist allegations in the modern sense.

A case in point is the allegations against supposed witches. In medieval times, these were directed almost exclusively at individuals; it was not until the early modern period, from around the middle of the fifteenth century, that the notion of large-scale witch conspiracies gradually developed throughout Europe, reaching a tragic climax in a series of pogroms in the seventeenth century before dying down again. In this context, Werner Tschacher rightly points to a 'qualitative leap in the development of sophisticated conspiracy theories' which he attributes partly to the new complexity of witchcraft, 'its specific combination of irrationality and rationality', and the 'use of modern media'.[6] Information on witches' alleged activities and how to identify them was circulated among European clerics in a number of tracts and treatises, such as Nicholas Jacquier's *Flagellum haereticorum fascinariorum* of 1458. Here, then, was a new reading public – albeit a very limited one – among whom theories about the nature of witches and their plots could be shared.

Where this conspiracy theory differs from ancient and most subsequent conspiracy theories is, of course, in its metaphysical character. In this case, it is not just human agents who are involved: the witches are led by the Devil, who, according to the Christian belief, is ultimately controlled by God. For this reason, witch conspiracies were often interpreted as a divine punishment. 'God indeed has the Devil in a *Chain*, but has horribly lengthened out the *Chain*', the Puritan Cotton Mather wrote at the height of the Salem witch trials of 1692, assuring readers that there was still hope as long as God had not let go of the chain entirely.[7]

It was not so much the Devil, but rather the Antichrist who figured in the conspiracy allegations that followed during the Wars of Religion sparked by the Reformation and the division of the Church. According to the historians Cornel Zwierlein and Beatrice de Graaf, the numerous accusations of collusion with the Devil levelled by either side in the conflict were the first full-blown conspiracy theories since ancient times, in the sense that they were complex narratives circulated in a public arena created by the printing press and motivated by the need to make sense of an ever more complex world. Within the complicated European state structure, it had grown increasingly difficult to identify the centres of power; even the Pope or the Emperor could no longer be relied on to be in full control. In this situation, conspiracy theories became an important means of imposing order on the perceived chaos. This new function is also reflected in a semantic shift: from around 1560 onwards, the hitherto rarely used terms *conspiratio* and *conspiracy* and their derivatives became an increasingly important element of the political language of Europe.[8]

As an integral part of political discourse, conspiracy theories constituted perfectly legitimate knowledge in the early modern period, just as they had done in antiquity. They were believed and propagated by the elites and the masses alike, and their basic assumptions were not doubted. Even the secularization process ushered in by the Enlightenment did nothing to change this. It may have altered the conspiracy scenarios – which gradually dispensed with the Devil, Antichrist and witches, and became increasingly complex over the course of the seventeenth and eighteenth centuries – but not the potency of the theories themselves. On the contrary, since God was now no longer the one pulling the strings, and the models of the modern social sciences were not yet available, conspiracist explanations became even more attractive, as they allowed people to continue believing in an ordered world where there was no place for chaos and contingency.[9]

In an important essay from the early 1980s, the historian Gordon Wood already showed how the popularity of conspiracy theories in the eighteenth century sprang from their ability to encapsulate the general vision of leading Enlightenment figures, who posited 'a world of mechanistic cause and effect' where all 'actions and events could now be seen scientifically as the products of men's intentions'. Based on this direct connection, thinkers such as John Locke concluded that 'Good intentions and beliefs would therefore result in good actions; evil motives caused evil actions.' Coincidences and unintended consequences were not completely ruled out, but they were the exception: 'a series of events that seemed to form a pattern could be no accident'. By the same token, the intentions of an individual or group could be inferred from their actions, even when expressly denied. This world view lends itself ideally to the conspiracist mode of deduction. Accordingly, throughout the eighteenth century '[t]he belief in plots was not a symptom of disturbed minds but a rational attempt to explain human phenomena in terms of human intentions and to maintain moral coherence in the affairs of men'.[10]

This is how Wood explains the prominence of conspiracy theories around the time of the American War of Independence. Founding fathers like George Washington, Thomas Jefferson or John Adams were convinced that the North American colonies were the victim of a conspiracy by the English king and his ministers, and this belief was a decisive factor in the lead-up to the revolution. At the same time, Wood also maintains that conspiracism rapidly lost credibility towards the end of the eighteenth century and shifted from the mainstream to the fringes of society. On this point, Geoffrey Cubitt, who has studied conspiracy theories in nineteenth-century France, remarks with very British understatement: 'Quite simply, this recession shows very little sign of having happened during the nineteenth and early twentieth centuries.'[11]

Indeed, the status of conspiracy theories remained unchanged until well into the twentieth century in Europe and North America; up to that point, they circulated as legitimate knowledge among the emerging public spheres on both continents. From George Washington to Dwight D. Eisenhower, there probably never was an American president who did not believe in conspiracy theories. Likewise, the brief text from Winston Churchill quoted at the beginning of this book shows how firmly entrenched conspiracist thinking was among the British elites in the first half of the twentieth century. And in Germany, renowned author and Nobel Laureate Thomas Mann wrote as late as 1918, in his *Reflections of a Nonpolitical Man*:

> Historical research will reveal what role the international *illuminati*, the world lodge of Freemasons, excluding, of course, the unsuspecting Germans, has played in the intellectual preparation and actual unleashing of the World War, the war of 'civilization' *against Germany*. As for me, even before there was any evidence, I had my own exact and irrefutable convictions about this.[12]

Thus, conspiracy theories remained hugely influential from the eighteenth until well into the twentieth century. The theory that Freemasons and the Illuminati had orchestrated the French Revolution and were planning further plots spread quickly throughout Europe via the writings of Barruel, Starck and John Robison and also reached the USA, where the fear of an intrigue by these groups against the young republic led to the passing of the 1798 Alien and Sedition Acts – four laws limiting the rights of foreigners and granting the president sweeping powers to take action against allegedly subversive criticism of the executive. A few decades later, the previously discussed conspiracy theory that European Catholic powers were bent on destroying the USA achieved great popularity. It even led to the founding of a new party, the so-called Know-Nothing Party, which only failed to win the 1856 presidential elections because its members were split over the issue of slavery. And the founding myth of the Republican Party, whose 1860 election victory sparked the Civil War, was the conspiracy theory that the so-called Slave Power was seeking to extend slavery to the whole of the USA. Even after that war had ended, conspiracy theories were still rife, and conspiracist allegations continued to command influence, from the mass protests by farmers in the west of the country during the final decades of the nineteenth century (which, incidentally, gave rise to the term 'populism'), to the communist witch-hunt after the Second World War.[13]

In Europe, it was the same story. During the course of the nineteenth century, all kinds of groups – first the Freemasons again, then the socialists and later the communists – came under suspicion of plotting to destroy the political order. Just as in the case of the rumours surrounding the French Revolution, these groups were regularly accused of collaborating in secret. In Germany, the Catholics were also targeted by conservative conspiracy theorists, while in Catholic France the allegations had to be more specific, and were thus directed against the Jesuits. In the decades leading up to the First World War, conspiracist suspicions then began to focus increasingly on the Jews. This development reached its tragic climax in the Nazi extermination camps, which would not have been possible without the spectre of a global Jewish conspiracy. Conversely, however, it was the experience of the Holocaust that – combined with other factors – led to the rapid delegitimization and stigmatization of conspiracy theories after the Second World War.[14]

Delegitimization and stigmatization after 1945

At first sight, the observation that conspiracy theories have enjoyed less popularity and influence in recent decades than in the preceding decades and centuries will inevitably appear counterintuitive. After all, in the age of the coronavirus, reports about COVID-19 conspiracy theories are in the news almost every day and, as demonstrated by the numerous surveys cited in the introduction, a significant proportion of the population in the USA and Europe currently believes in conspiracy theories. Unsurprisingly, therefore, several scholars have argued that such theories have moved increasingly to the forefront of social discourse over the last few years, giving them ever greater influence. In my view, however, the opposite is true. Most media coverage is concerned with conspiracy *theories*, not conspiracies, the underlying assumption being that people see or claim to see plots where none in fact exist. In a sense, conspiracism is like sexism or racism: while such attitudes have by no means disappeared – there are still plenty of sexists, racists and conspiracy theorists around – they attract much more attention than in the past, precisely because they are no longer perceived as normal, but rather as problematic and sometimes even dangerous. In short, whereas we used to be afraid of conspiracies, we are now more afraid of conspiracy theories.[15]

In the case of the USA, this impression is borne out by the study conducted by Joseph Uscinski and Joseph Parent who, in a quantitative survey based partly on readers' letters to major newspapers, noted a decline in conspiracist suspicions after the mid-1960s: 'From 1964 on, conspiracy theories average half a percent of the letters per year, while before 1964 conspiracy theories are more than double. The data suggest one telling fact: we do not live in an age of conspiracy theories and have not for some time.' In the case of the UK, Andrew McKenzie-McHarg and Rolf Fredheim, who spent many years on the research project 'Conspiracy and Democracy' at the University of Cambridge, have demonstrated the same development in a very interesting study. The two researchers took the digital recordings of UK parliamentary debates from 1916 to 2015 and subjected them to a quantitative analysis. In the early debates, there are frequent mentions of 'conspiracy' but none of 'conspiracy theory'. After 1965, however, the ratio gradually reverses, until conspiracy allegations hardly figure at all. In the rare event that such an allegation is made, the response is invariably to dismiss the claim as a conspiracy theory. In other words, the UK parliament – which can be safely assumed to mirror society in this respect – has seen an increasing problematization of conspiracy theories over the course of the last century.[16]

In this sense, the UK and the USA typify the evolution that conspiracy theories have undergone in Europe and North America. If we compare the discourse on conspiracies and conspiracy theories in the countries of these regions in the early twentieth and early twenty-first centuries, it soon becomes clear that the process of delegitimization and stigmatization has occurred throughout this part of the world, and that conspiracy theories have developed from orthodox to heterodox knowledge. How and why this change has taken place is not nearly as clear, however. For the USA, Katharina Thalmann has recently traced this development in great detail, and it is safe to assume that similar factors have been at work in Europe.[17]

Thalmann argues that conspiracist beliefs were first problematized by social scientists in the USA, and that this gradually seeped into Americans' everyday consciousness. The delegitimization process takes place in three phases: in the 1930s, there is a need to explain the causes of totalitarianism in Europe; after the Second World War, research is motivated by the communist witch-hunt at home; and in the 1960s, the issue is taken up by the so-called consensus historians around Richard Hofstadter, who see American society as characterized by a broad commitment to liberalism and democracy. It also takes place from two different perspectives, the more psychological approaches concentrating on the psychopathology of conspiracy theorists, and the more epistemological ones on the gaps and contradictions in their arguments.[18]

The first phase of this process is dominated by what Thalmann calls the 'Frankfurt School of conspiracy theory'. She is referring here to Theodor W. Adorno and Leo Löwenthal, two exponents of the Frankfurt School living in exile in America who, along with the political scientist Harold Lasswell, first began to study conspiracy theories, thereby shaping the early discourse on the subject. In a series of papers produced up to the early 1950s, Lasswell and the German exiles researched the psychological causes of totalitarianism and its characteristic tendency to see conspiracies everywhere. Lasswell was interested in the motives and rhetoric of the agitator; Adorno wrote *The Authoritarian Personality*, in which he coined the term 'paranoid style' later adopted by Richard Hofstadter; and Löwenthal co-wrote *Prophets of Deceit* with the Polish-born scholar Norbert Guterman. All these studies are essentially concerned with how charismatic leaders – the figure of Hitler looming inevitably in the background – take social problems and distort them as a result of their own psychological disposition in a way that encourages the emergence of large-scale conspiracy scenarios peddling simple solutions to complicated problems.[19]

From the 1940s onwards, conspiracist thinking is criticized from another angle by Karl Popper. As already discussed in Chapter 1, rather than analysing the psychology of conspiracy theorists, Popper's critique focuses on the epistemological bases of their argumentation. For Popper, conspiracy theories cannot be correct because they place far too much emphasis on the ability of human beings to put their intentions into practice, without taking into account systemic constraints and unintended consequences. Like Lasswell, Adorno and Löwenthal, however, Popper also insists on the danger of conspiracy theories. And in *The Open Society and Its Enemies*, he is the first to use the term 'conspiracy theory' in its modern sense.[20]

The studies from this initial phase of delegitimization failed to find much of an audience beyond the ivory tower of academia, however, and hence made no impact on the wider public. In the 1950s, by contrast, the pioneers' ideas were taken up and developed by a new generation of researchers. Scholars such as the sociologist Edward Shils or the political scientist Seymour Martin Lipset switched their attention from totalitarianism in Europe to the situation in the USA, where many left-wing and liberal intellectuals were coming increasingly under suspicion of being part of a communist plot. To rebut these accusations, academics either tackled the conspiracy theorists in the Frankfurt School manner, branding them 'pseudo-conservative' or 'populist', or they took the Popperist line, attacking their pattern of reasoning and exposing them as 'pseudoscientific'. Unlike the work of Adorno or Popper, these studies attracted notice beyond the bounds of academia. This was due partly to the efforts of Shils, Lipset and their ilk to adopt an accessible style that would reach a wider public, and partly to the emergence of a number of willing multipliers outside universities. Many journalists also regarded the Red Scare conspiracy theories as a danger to American democracy and therefore seized on the research findings, thereby helping to popularize them.[21]

The effects of this process soon became apparent. Having been firmly anchored in mainstream society in the early 1950s, the anti-communist conspiracy theory soon drifted into subcultures, so that, ten years on, only members of the far-right John Birch Society and similar groups continued to believe in the communist plot to undermine American institutions. In turn, the popularity of conspiracy theories among extremists led to a growing tendency in the academic debate of the 1960s and 1970s to claim a natural affinity between radical positions at the margins of society and conspiracist ideology. For consensus historians like John Bunzel, who emphasized the importance of pluralism, extremist positions were not only anti-democratic, but also anti-political, due in large part to the prominence of conspiracy theories. This stance culminated in Richard Hofstadter's famous essay 'The Paranoid Style in American Politics', which I have already mentioned several times. Hofstadter took the pathologization of conspiracy theories to extremes by equating them with clinical paranoia, and marginalized such ideas by mistakenly claiming that, historically, they had never been more than a minority phenomenon on the fringes of US society. The fact that Hofstadter's essay was first published in the popular *Harper's Magazine* shows just how widespread this stance had become within the space of a few years.[22]

This development was reinforced by another factor that Thalmann also discusses. Not only were the ideas of Lasswell, Lipset and Hofstadter catching on outside universities; after the Second World War, more and more Americans were also going to university. Under the G.I. Bill of 1944, demobbed soldiers were able to go to college. For soldiers from low income and ethnic groups who had previously been denied the chance to study, this represented a great opportunity, and many took advantage of it. Later on, the law was extended to veterans of the Korean War and then to all members of the US forces. Due to the structure of American college education, the first two years of which are spent attending classes in a variety of disciplines, large numbers of students are therefore likely to have come into contact with studies explicitly critiquing conspiracist thinking, or nuanced social science models emphasizing structural constraints over human agency.

At this point, it is important to briefly address a powerful argument made by the French sociologist and philosopher of science Bruno Latour. Anticipating the challenges to scientific consensus on climate change and other contested issues from fake news, the dismissal of epistemic authorities and the spreading of what Donald Trump's adviser Kellyanne Conway later smugly called 'alternative facts', he wrote an essay as early as 2004 pondering the question 'Has critique run out of steam?' More specifically, Latour detects an uncanny resemblance between nuanced social theory and conspiracy theory, since both focus on 'powerful agents hidden in the dark'. 'Of course', he concedes,

> we in the academy like to use more elevated causes – society, discourse, knowledge-slash-power, fields of forces, empires, capitalism – while conspiracists like to portray a miserable bunch of greedy people with dark intents, but I find something troublingly similar in the structure of the explanation, in the first movement of disbelief and, then, in the wheeling of causal explanations coming out of the deep dark below.

In other words, Latour worries that the social sciences have paved the way for an unprecedented number of conspiracy theories, and that the language of social constructivism has fuelled conspiracist rhetoric.[23]

Latour certainly has a point here. In the last few years in particular, conspiracy theorists have referred to the insights of social constructivism whenever it suited them. However, because he is not aware of the historical development of conspiracy theories and their stigmatization in the Western world in the second half of the twentieth century, Latour confuses cause and consequence. If the rhetoric and argumentative structure of social analyses is often strikingly similar to that of conspiracy theories – a fact also highlighted by Peter Knight – it is not because the social sciences have given rise to conspiracy theories, but because they replaced conspiracy theories as the legitimate way of explaining how the world works. They replaced the focus on intentional actions with a focus on abstract forces and systemic factors. At the same time, the fact that they could not quite shed the rhetoric of conspiracism is an important indicator of the enduring attraction and appeal of conspiracy theories despite their stigmatization.[24]

It would therefore be a big mistake to assume that stigmatization led to a virtual disappearance of conspiracy theories. For one thing, the delegitimization process was confined to North America and Europe; in other parts of the world, conspiracy theories remain an entirely legitimate form of knowledge to this day. And even in places where they have become heterodox knowledge, they have not lost their attraction. Although they have fewer adherents than in earlier decades due to the stigma now attached to them, numerous studies have shown that conspiracy theories still enjoy a high degree of popularity. Until a few years ago, however (and these latest developments are the subject of the next chapter), many people would not have openly admitted to this precisely because conspiracy theories are no longer acceptable in public discourse. In academic discourse, the media and political communications (the exception of Donald Trump is also explored in the next chapter), they are almost always presented as a problem or danger.

As of the past few decades, therefore, those who continue to believe in conspiracy theories or spread them for some ulterior motive have two options open to them, as Katharina Thalmann has demonstrated. They can either try to maintain their mainstream appeal by rejecting the label 'conspiracy theorist' and claiming instead to be simply asking questions, or they can consciously accept their marginal status and make a virtue of it. This is generally done by formulating superconspiracy theories which merge together multiple scenarios, and which assume society to be so firmly in the hands of the conspirators that the only way to bring the truth to light and find an audience for it is through subcultures and alternative public spheres. Thus, we have seen two kinds of conspiracy theory develop around every major event since the assassination of Kennedy: the kind exemplified by Edward Epstein, who claimed to be simply criticizing the official version of events; and the kind articulated by Jim Garrison in his attempt to prove that the CIA, the FBI, the military and other agents were all behind the assassination. With regard to 9/11, there are likewise conspiracy theorists like Daniele Ganser, who say they are only asking questions, and conspiracy theorists like Alex Jones, who actively promote the view that the attacks were carried out on behalf of the New World Order.[25]

It is doubtless no coincidence that, since their stigmatization in 'serious' discourse, conspiracy scenarios have grown increasingly popular in films, television series and novels. One feature that distinguishes media products such as the novels of Robert Ludlum or David Baldacci, films like *Salt* (2010) or the Jason Bourne series and TV series like *The Americans* (2013–18) or *Stranger Things* (2016–) from the conspiracy claims of people like Alex Jones or David Icke is that, within their fictional worlds, the plots are not merely alleged, but undeniably real. In other words, fiction routinely stages conspiracies. For those members of the public who are already inclined towards conspiracism, such narratives may confirm their assumptions, while those who don't believe in the feasibility of vast plots in reality can indulge their fantasy safe in the knowledge that the fictitious scenarios fall into the category of 'nonserious discourse'.[26]

At the same time, fiction also reflects the change in status that conspiracy theories have undergone since the late 1950s. Alongside films and novels in which the conspiracy is presented as real, there are plenty of texts which are best described not as conspiracy thrillers but as conspiracy *theory* thrillers. Films such as *The Parallax View* (1974), *Winter Kills* (1979) or *Conspiracy Theory* (1997), in which Mel Gibson plays a taxi driver afflicted by delusions, focus more on their protagonists' doubts about whether the conspiracy in question really exists than on the machinations of the conspiracy itself. The answer is left hanging in the air until the end – and sometimes beyond – thereby encouraging the viewer to reflect on the conditions that make conspiracies possible and the attraction as well as the problems of conspiracist paradigms. This technique is carried to extremes in Thomas Pynchon's novel *The Crying of Lot 49* (1966), which ends just as we are finally about to learn whether the protagonist is suffering from paranoia or has genuinely uncovered a plot.

A somewhat different method is employed in the bestsellers by Dan Brown. His protagonist Robert Langdon is invariably sceptical to begin with, but comes to accept that there really is a conspiracy involving the Illuminati, Freemasons or the Catholic Church, and only realizes in the last few pages that the conspiracy was merely staged in order to deceive him and everyone else, and that there is a single perpetrator behind all the crimes. In this sense, Brown's novels have more in common with the postmodern experiments of Pynchon or Don DeLillo than the thrillers of Ludlum or Baldacci. By suggesting initially to the reader that a major conspiracy is afoot within the fictional world and then revealing it to be an illusion, they reflect the present status of conspiracy theories, i.e. they have not lost their appeal, but neither do they allow an adequate understanding of reality.[27]

Case study: the myth of the global Jewish conspiracy

Conspiracy allegations against Jews are well-suited to illustrate the developments outlined so far in this chapter, as they have a long history and – at least since the early twentieth century – a global currency. Moreover, due to its terrible consequences for the accused, this particular conspiracy theory has been relatively well researched both in terms of the recent and more distant past. That said, our knowledge of the destruction of the European Jews under the Nazis has also led to a tendency within anti-Semitism research to see a long, linear trend stretching back to the Middle Ages and leading continuously to the Holocaust, which is not in fact the case.[28]

As Johannes Heil has shown, early incarnations and stock themes of subsequent global conspiracy theories have existed throughout Europe since the late Middle Ages, although these still differ significantly from conspiracy theories as I understand them here. The allegations in question are often of limited scope and reach, such as the story peddled by Bernardino Zambotti that Jews had 'slaughtered' a small boy in Venice in 1480. And even when the scenarios are more ambitious – as in Matthew of Paris's account of Jews joining forces with the Tartars and attempting to smuggle weapons into France in wine casks, a plot only discovered by chance during a routine inspection – there is a critical difference between these and conspiracy theories in the proper sense: Matthew and many other chroniclers of the time only ever reported on plots that had already been foiled, never on ongoing conspiracies that needed to be tackled by mobilizing allies. Moreover, there was no public arena in which to circulate such texts; whether they played a role in verbal communication is impossible to say. The example of the destruction of the Templar Order in the early fourteenth century suggests that there is indeed a conceptual difference between these medieval forms and conspiracy theories in the narrow sense. Although the persecution of the Knights Templar continued for some years until the conclusion of the last trials and the dissolution of the order in 1312, generating a good deal of literature in the process, conspiracy allegations only began to appear in 'the subsequent historiography'.[29]

This began to change in the fourteenth century, however. During the plague epidemic that swept gradually northwards across Europe from the mid-1340s, costing the lives of a significant part of the population, anti-Jewish conspiracy theories began to circulate which already bore a close resemblance to modern ones. As the epidemic continued to spread, voices were raised in many places blaming the Jews and accusing them of poisoning the wells. Not only were they made a scapegoat of in order to explain something that was otherwise inexplicable, they were also accused of seeking to destroy the Christian community in order to seize power. In contrast to the conspiracy theories that have emerged since the early modern period, however, no evidence was provided for these accusations, or for the plan allegedly behind the deeds; people simply referred to the malicious character of the Jews.[30]

Interestingly, accusations against Jews tailed off dramatically with the beginning of the early modern period. They could still resurface at any time, because the stock themes were familiar and hence readily available. But in the fifteenth and sixteenth centuries – just when modern-style conspiracy theories were emerging, and witch-hunts were on the rise and increasingly linked to conspiracies – they were resorted to much less frequently. This may be to do with the fact that, in the wake of the Reformation, other enemy stereotypes came to the fore and were deployed in a conspiracist context; alternatively, it may be due to the increasing secularization of conspiracy scenarios, resulting in a greater focus on actors in the political arena, where Jews were devoid of any influence.[31]

There is, therefore, no line of continuity between the anti-Jewish allegations of the Middle Ages and the anti-Semitic global conspiracy theories of modern times in the sense of a religious pattern that gradually became secularized. On the contrary, conspiracy allegations against Jews in Europe only regained popularity and influence during the nineteenth century, in the wake of the conspiracy theories that sprang up around the French Revolution and which progressively expanded to include Catholics, socialists and other groups besides the Illuminati and Freemasons. Around 1795, the first texts were published that characterized Jews, if not as the masterminds, then certainly as the beneficiaries of a rebellion orchestrated by other subversive forces in France. An early sign of this change was the 'Simonini letter' addressed to Augustin Barruel, author of the conspiracist *Memoirs Illustrating the History of Jacobinism*. In it, a Florentine captain named Jean-Baptiste Simonini begins by congratulating Barruel on exposing the driving forces behind the French Revolution, but goes on to criticize him for completely ignoring the key role of the Jews. Although Barruel himself made no changes to this effect in the new editions of his book, the Jews became increasingly pivotal to conservative conspiracy theories in Central and Western Europe over the course of the nineteenth century, to the point that 'the attributes "Masonic" and "Jewish" became equivalent, indeed interchangeable terms'.[32] The reason why the Jews never fully replaced the Freemasons in these texts was presumably that the secret society was initially perceived by many readers as much more dangerous; the alleged threat from the Jews was more by association.

This also explains why, in the most important text on the global Jewish conspiracy to date, *The Protocols of the Elders of Zion*, the Jews are again lumped together with the Freemasons. The *Protocols*, whose authorship is still disputed, claim to be the authentic records of a meeting between the leaders of international Jewry where plans for world domination were openly discussed. They are, as discussed in Chapter 2, a complete fabrication, yet they are still regarded – even by many who accept that they are a forgery – as evidence of a large-scale Jewish plot. Accordingly, one might expect a conglomeration of all the anti-Jewish tropes passed down from the Middle Ages (ritual murder, well poisonings, desecration of the host, etc.). However, since the *Protocols* are written in the tradition of conservative conspiracist literature on the French Revolution, they make no mention of these. Only the so-called Marx-Rothschild theorem – which places Jews on either side of the intensifying class struggle, as both capitalists and communist agitators – features in the text, because it fits the ideology of a work driven by the fear of upheaval and rebellion.[33]

As such, the popularity of the *Protocols* stems from the fact that they were never disseminated in standalone form, but always embedded in and sometimes completely eclipsed by paratexts of various kinds. According to Eva Horn, 'it is the prefaces, explanatory notes and commentaries ... that (particularly after the First World War) trigger the stringently racist, anti-Semitic response', building as they do on familiar anti-Semitic motifs such as well poisonings and host desecration. As Horn has conclusively argued, this was a case of 'reception without reading': people merely skimmed the text itself, if at all, and homed in on the prefaces and commentaries, which deliberately linked individual ideas from the *Protocols* to culturally and regionally specific contemporary events. This was nearly always possible given the document's failure to present any coherent picture of the Jewish plans. Sometimes the takeover of power is described as imminent, and sometimes as far in the future; sometimes it is to be achieved by violent revolution, and sometimes by cunning and deceit. It is therefore quite possible that the text – if not originally conceived as a satire on anti-Jesuit conspiracy theories – was intended by its authors to be received in exactly that spirit. This would also be consistent with the logic of conspiracist arguments as discussed in Chapter 2. As a supposedly confidential document leaked to the public, the *Protocols* are a powerful piece of evidence. Like all evidence, however, they have to be integrated into a specific conspiracy narrative. Thus, individual passages are cited in the prefaces and the whole text becomes an appendix to the introduction, in which the actual conspiracy theory is expounded.[34]

After the First World War in particular, which, seen through the prism of the text, could be interpreted as a Jewish plot, the *Protocols* exerted a huge influence on many people's understanding of the world, especially – though not exclusively – in Germany, where the book was first published in translation in 1920. In a detailed account, Wolfram Meyer zu Uptrup has demonstrated the extent to which the *Protocols* shaped the world view of Hitler and other leading Nazis, such as their chief ideologue Alfred Rosenberg. Although there were no new editions of the text after 1939 – perhaps because the vision of Jewish world domination centring on a messianic leader, as developed in the final pages, came dangerously close to the Nazi utopia – many of its ideas became a constant refrain of Nazi propaganda in newspapers such as the *Völkische Beobachter* and the weekly *Der Stürmer*. In this way, the *Protocols* helped to create a climate whose ultimate consequence was the genocide of European Jews.[35]

After 1945, overt anti-Semitism soon became stigmatized in large parts of the Western world due to the experience of the Holocaust. At the same time, the delegitimization and marginalization of conspiracist knowledge described in the previous section in relation to the USA was also happening in Europe. Since then – particularly in Germany – statements that present *The Protocols of the Elders of Zion* in a positive light no longer have a place in public discourse. One example of this was the controversy in summer 2016 surrounding Wolfgang Gedeon, a politician belonging to the right-wing populist Alternative for Germany (AfD). The public became aware of Gedeon's anti-Semitic writings after he was elected to parliament in the Baden-Württemberg state elections, in which the AfD won 15.7 per cent of the vote. In the second volume of his 2009 monograph *Christlicheuropäische Leitkultur. Die Herausforderung Europas durch Säkularismus, Zionismus und Islam* ['Mainstream European Christian culture: The challenge to Europe from secularism, Zionism and Islam'], and again, three years later, in *Der grüne Kommunismus und die Diktatur der Minderheiten* ['Green communism and the dictatorship of minorities'], he presented the *Protocols* not as the fake propaganda they really are, but as a reputable source. As public pressure to distance itself from Gedeon grew, the AfD group within the state parliament threatened to split, until Gedeon eventually left. Even within the AfD, positive references to the *Protocols* are still (as yet) taboo – at least in public. Behind closed doors and in the echo chambers of the internet it's a different story.[36]

In other parts of the world, by contrast, the *Protocols* remain a regular feature of public discourse. In the Arab world, for example, they have been known ever since the beginning of the twentieth century, having been introduced along with other anti-Masonic literature, or through the medium of Nazi propaganda. At first, though, the work was mainly read by members of the Christian minorities; it wasn't until 1950 that the first Arabic edition appeared.[37] In other words, the *Protocols* began to exert their influence in this part of the world just as they were becoming increasingly stigmatized in Europe. Their enduring popularity is attributable partly to the anti-Semitism that remains widespread in Arab countries to this day (fuelled, above all, by the unresolved Israeli-Palestinian conflict), and partly to the fact that conspiracy theories are still regarded as orthodox knowledge in this region. As a result, conspiracist rhetoric – most, though not all of it, anti-Semitic – is par for the course in public discourse, from parliaments to editorials to popular culture. In 2002, for example, the forty-one-part series *Horseman Without a Horse*, which is based on the *Protocols*, was shown on Egyptian TV; the following year, Lebanese TV followed suit with the series *Diaspora* – also based on the *Protocols* but much more brutal.[38]

Even in the Western world, the *Protocols* did not of course disappear altogether after 1945. Being no longer acceptable in public discourse, however – like anti-Semitic conspiracy theory in general – they were relegated to counterpublics and subcultures. In this way, ideas from the *Protocols* and other anti-Semitic conspiracy texts have become a fixture of conspiracy theories about the so-called New World Order, which can be traced back ultimately to the British author Nesta Webster. Over the last few decades in particular, this theory has attracted large numbers of followers in North America and Europe, the most high-profile being, without doubt, Alex Jones. There are now various versions of the theory in existence, but they all basically claim that transnational organizations such as the UN or the EU are being used by a small group of conspirators to abolish the sovereignty of national states and establish a world government under the noses of their populations. The conspirators are said to deploy all kinds of methods – from vaccinations through chemtrails to gender ideology – in order to weaken and subjugate the people.

Not all versions of the New World Order theory are overtly anti-Semitic, but almost all suggest such interpretations to those sections of their audience who are looking for them, by picking up on motifs from anti-Semitic conspiracist traditions without explicitly mentioning Jews. Thus, Donald Trump's allegation that Hillary Clinton met 'in secret with international banks to plot the destruction of US sovereignty' can be taken as a hint that the whole thing was being masterminded by Jews. Jews, after all, have been subject since medieval times to insinuations that they are homeless and hence international, have a close affinity to money, and benefit disproportionately from the international financial system. The same goes for the image of the 'EU octopus' driven by the financial system, which we encountered for example in the article on the refugee crisis by the former German news presenter Eva Herman. Here again, we are implicitly reminded of the strong association of Jews with money and (via the EU) internationality; furthermore, the octopus is a common metaphor for the alleged Jewish conspiracy that was frequently used in Nazi propaganda. Since neither Trump nor Herman accuse Jews directly of conspiracy, however, they are able to reject the allegation of anti-Semitism. Both would probably insist that their criticisms are directed not at an ethnic group, but at a corrupt elite. This brings us, finally, to the topic of populism.[39]

Conspiracy theories and populism

The close link between populism and conspiracism, though frequently noted, has so far rarely been the subject of any systematic discussion. Studies on conspiracy theories make regular reference to their populist dimension, while articles on populism often mention the prominence of conspiracy theories in populist discourse. Jan-Werner Müller, for example, states in *What Is Populism?* that '[c]onspiracy theories are ... not a curious addition to populist rhetoric; they are rooted in and emerge from the very logic of populism itself'. But he does not develop this idea at all. On the contrary, this sentence marks the end of a paragraph while the next is devoted to a completely different topic. This is typical of the literature touching on the relationship from the perspective of populism research. And the subject is dealt with even more perfunctorily by those engaged in conspiracy theory research (with one exception, which I will come to in a moment). Thus, Jovan Byford mentions in his introduction to conspiracy theories that allegations that Barack Obama was not born in the USA and was therefore not eligible to be president 'quickly became an important element in right-wing populist propaganda', but he does not pursue the point any further. To quote Kirk Hawkins and Cristóbal Rovira Kaltwasser, 'Despite the fact that various scholars have pointed out the link between populism and conspiratorial thinking ..., there is a dearth of empirical research on this argument.' Moreover, we could add, the relationship needs to be theorized more thoroughly than it has been so far.[40]

This is a difficult task, however, because populism is a highly contested concept. While there is a broad consensus on the definition of conspiracy theory that I am using in this book, there is far less unity on the question of what populism is and what it does. To the neo-Marxist Ernesto Laclau, populism is a necessary element of representative democracy that arises whenever the divide between the people and their representatives is felt to be too great. According to this

reading, populism is an answer to a crisis of political repre-
sentation which can – and this is where Laclau's definition
differs most significantly from others – be both detrimental
and conducive to democracy. As such, populism ultimately
has no substance of its own; rather, it is a particular method
of political mobilization that cannot be evaluated in general
terms, but only on a case-by-case basis. Müller, on the other
hand, emphasizes the anti-democratic nature of populism.
Because populists claim to know the true will of the people;
because they therefore regularly refuse to accept the results
of democratic elections; and because, once in power, they
routinely bypass democratic procedures, he does not see
populism in any way as 'a corrective to liberal democracy
in the sense of bringing politics "closer to the people" or
"reasserting popular sovereignty"', but quite the opposite.[41]

Although most of the more recent definitions do not go
quite as far as Müller's, they do paint – doubtless influenced by the upsurge of right-wing populism in the USA
and Europe – a much more negative picture of populism
than Laclau's, whose understanding of the phenomenon
was shaped by the undeniably emancipatory force of South
American movements.[42] These definitions insist that the
assertion of an antagonistic relationship between the people
and the elite is fundamental to populism, however differently
the two poles may be perceived. This opposition is, moreover,
morally charged, with the elite being accused of ignoring the
interests of the people or acting deliberately against their will.
Populist politicians claim to know – by whatever means –
what that will is. In their eyes, they are the ones articulating
what Rousseau called the *volonté generale*. In this, they are
aided by the notion that not every eligible voter or inhabitant
of a country belongs to 'the people'. After the extremely
close result of the Brexit referendum, the then leader of the
Eurosceptic UKIP party, Nigel Farage, hailed it as a 'victory
for real people'.[43] In other words, populists regard those
who they do not count among the people as illegitimate – a
decidedly anti-pluralist stance.

The most obvious parallel between populism and
conspiracy theories is their mistrust of elites.[44] I should
qualify this statement immediately, however, by saying that
it only applies to contemporary conspiracy theories. As long

as conspiracy theories were a wholly legitimate form of knowledge and were articulated mainly by elites, it was very rare for them to be directed against other elites; in most cases, they targeted 'bottom-up' adversaries: Jesuits in nineteenth-century France, Catholics in the USA, and socialists, followed by communists, in Germany. It was only after conspiracy theories became illegitimate knowledge that this changed. Nowadays, conspiracy theories are frowned upon and can no longer be propagated in elite discourse, at least not overtly. Because they persist outside the mainstream, however, at the margins of society, their target has switched accordingly. Since the 1960s, most conspiracy allegations have been aimed at 'top-down' adversaries, i.e. political elites such as the government, institutions such as intelligence services or the military, and financial elites. The clearest parallel between conspiracy theories and populism does not, therefore, exist regardless of time or place, but only in the context of the specific historical constellation of (neo)liberal democracy condemned by populists, and the stigmatization of conspiracism by elite discourses.

This does not mean, of course, that populists can no longer resort to conspiracy theories once in power. On the contrary: it is part of the standard repertoire of populist heads of state and their supporters to denounce the alleged plots of elites who cling to their privileges despite the fact that the people have chosen an entirely different direction by democratic election. Thus, Hugo Chávez justified a string of measures during his presidency of Venezuela by claiming that large parts of the system such as health care were still in the hands of conspiratorial elites. And in the USA and Turkey respectively, many supporters of Presidents Trump and Erdoğan are now accusing the so-called deep state, that is, the bureaucratic elites of their countries, of boycotting their leaders' reform plans. Such claims are often accompanied by allegations of collaboration between internal elites and powerful enemies outside the country. The main target of Chávez's attacks on this front was the CIA which, in light of its notorious history in South America, was (and still is) felt by many to be capable of involvement in a (further) plot. Similarly, Hungary's right-wing populist Fidesz Party has focused for some years now on the American investment banker and philanthropist George Soros. Prime Minister Victor Orbán routinely accuses him of secretly pursuing a plan to destabilize the political order in Hungary via his charitable foundations. It is therefore also conceivable that populist leaders might level conspiracy allegations at an internal, 'bottom-up' enemy, such as an ethnic minority. They would just need to accuse this group of being in league with a powerful external enemy who can take the place of the elite.[45]

But what else do conspiracy theories and populism have in common besides the critique of elites? The idea I am about to suggest builds on the groundwork done by Mark Fenster. In his book on conspiracy theories, Fenster describes conspiracist ideology as a 'non-necessary element' of populism. By this, he means that all contemporary conspiracy theories are essentially populist because they are directed against an elite of some kind, while some but not all populist movements are based on conspiracy theories. As should be clear from my previous remarks, I share the view that there is no 'natural' correlation between populism and conspiracy theories. Both *can* occur completely independently of each other, but they are commonly encountered – at least in their current forms – in combination.[46]

Therefore I would modify Fenster's thesis as follows: conspiracy theories offer a specific explanation as to why the elites act against the interests of the people. This explanation tends to coexist within a populist movement or party with other explanations such as negligence or personal enrichment. In other words, conspiracy theories are a non-necessary element of populist discourse and ideology, and they are not necessarily believed by everybody in the populist movement or party in which they are circulating. However, populist movements are very good at integrating conspiracy theorists and non-conspiracy theorists. This is due to a number of structural and functional parallels between conspiracy theories and populism that make the only difference between them – i.e. that conspiracy theorists accuse elites of being part of a plot while other populists do not – appear relatively insignificant.

The key structural parallel lies in the fact that both populism and conspiracy theories radically simplify the political arena by reducing it to an extremely small number of actors. Both reject the assumption that a modern democracy involves a multiplicity of actors whose interests and intentions are sometimes mutually contradictory, and sometimes complementary. Instead, both populism and conspiracism work on the basis of just two groups with diametrically opposed interests. Steven van Hauwaert has called this the 'shared dualism' of populism and conspiracy theory. In the populist's world view, everything revolves around the conflict between the elite and the people; in the conspiracy theorist's, the opposition is between the conspirators and their victims. Populists identify those who have seen through the machinations of the elite and now oppose them as a subgroup of the people; conspiracy theorists see themselves as the ones who, having discovered the identity and motives of those secretly pulling the strings, are now seeking to educate the masses.[47]

For example, many of the conspiracy theories that fuelled the Brexit campaign claim that Brussels bureaucrats – and, for that matter, the EU as a whole – do not represent a variety of viewpoints based on nationality and political conviction. Instead, they are all allegedly plotting the disenfranchisement of the people, with the ultimate goal of abolishing national sovereignty and creating a European super-state. Before the referendum, moreover, there were conspiracy theories to the effect that the government was manipulating the voting process in favour of Remainers, thus effectively disregarding the will of the people. According to these allegations, government officials, despite publicly declaring otherwise, had a common position, and that position was diametrically opposed to what the people wanted. A similar accusation levelled not at the EU, but at the established parties in Germany, appears in the manifesto of the right-wing populist Alternative for Germany: 'Behind the scenes [in Germany] a small and powerful elite within the political parties is secretly in charge.' All other parties, then, are singing from the same hymn sheet while only the AfD represents a genuinely different stance, namely that of the people.[48]

A further parallel lies in the potential of both conspiracy theories and populism to be either left- or right-wing, or indeed to subvert these traditional categories. Common to both, however – as mentioned in the previous chapter – is an inherent conservatism. Both seek to preserve a threatened social order or restore one that has already been destroyed. Just think of Donald Trump's campaign slogans: 'Make America Great Again' in 2016 and 'Keep America Great' in 2020. Unsurprisingly, therefore, populism and conspiracy theory often share a nostalgia for a past that in most cases never actually existed – in the case of conspiracy theories, the time before the plot, and in that of populism, the time before the elites turned their back on the people. In both cases, the critique of the status quo is not always related to economic developments – although these can play a role, and were indeed a major factor in the South American populist movements – but is just as likely to be driven by the 'feeling of being left behind *culturally*'.[49] What matters most, therefore, is often not economics, but identity politics. The sense that there is no longer a place for traditional values and one's own life plan is a particularly strong motivating force behind the populist movements currently enjoying such a boom, and among whose membership conspiracy theories are rife. This also explains why – as already discussed at the end of the previous chapter – white men are more inclined than most to believe in conspiracy theories, and are currently leading the populist movements in North America and Europe. This demographic group has the most to lose, economically, culturally and socially.

A third parallel between conspiracy theories and populism, moreover, lies in their habit of looking on the dark side of the present but the bright side of the future, on the assumption that the conspiracies can be crushed or the elites disempowered. This optimistic aspect is something we have already seen in relation to conspiracy theories, and the same applies to populism. After all, if all ills result not from complex geopolitical developments or a shift in values deeply rooted in our own society, but from a plot or just the negligence of the elites, then the clock can be turned back, and the changes perceived as so negative and dangerous can be duly reversed.

Ultimately, then, conspiracy theories are just one way of explaining the behaviour of elites. It is not simply that they are out of touch, ideologically suspect, driven by personal gain, individually corrupt, plain stupid or even bound by structural constraints: they are actually betraying the interests of the people by serving other masters – in other words, they are part of a conspiracy. This is why populist movements can readily unite those who believe in a conspiracy of the elites and those who attribute their 'misconduct' to other causes. These different viewpoints have no impact on the practice of protest itself. When it comes to chanting slogans like 'Merkel must go!' or 'End the lockdown!', believers in conspiracy theories and non-believers can march side by side.

This observation is borne out by the few existing empirical studies on the spread of conspiracist beliefs in contemporary populist movements. One quantitative survey conducted during the Republican primaries, for example, showed that conspiracy theories were far more widespread among supporters of Donald Trump than among those of his competitors Ted Cruz and John Kasich. But never – even at this early stage of the election campaign, when the Republican establishment was still backing his inner-party rivals – did a majority of Trump fans believe in a specific conspiracy theory. This impression is also supported by the results of the qualitative study by Laura Luise Hammel, who conducted research into the role of conspiracy theories in new German social movements such as Pegida or the Vigils for Peace.[50]

The willingness of non-conspiracy theorists to demonstrate alongside conspiracy theorists may also have to do with the modern-day status of conspiracy theories. The very stigmatization of such theories in elite discourse can make them an attractive weapon of anti-elitist critique. Thus, the expression of conspiracist views can be understood as a conscious rejection of norms and conventions that are perceived as elitist in the literal sense of the word, whereby the emphasis may be less on the substance of those views than on the habitus they represent. That it is (still) possible to define oneself in this way is partly due to the fact that, despite the advent of the internet, conspiracy theories have not lost their status as illegitimate knowledge. As far as other aspects of conspiracist discourse are concerned, however, the internet has indeed been a significant force for change.[51]

5

Current trends, or: How is the internet changing conspiracy theories?

My argument so far that the legitimacy and hence also the popularity and influence of conspiracy theories in the Western world have declined in recent decades would appear to have a crucial weakness. While it may explain the virtual absence of conspiracist ideas from public discourse between, say, 1965 and 2000, my case is, on the face of it, utterly belied by the developments of the last twenty years. Indeed – as I myself observed in my introduction – we are now in an age where conspiracy theories are practically omnipresent. In summer 2016, the UK voted to leave the EU after a campaign marked by countless conspiracy theories surrounding migrants and the EU. A few months later, the USA elected a president who circulated all manner of conspiracy rumours on Twitter during his election campaign. And and the coronavirus pandemic has generated a plethora of conspiracy theories that have motivated people all over the world to take to the streets and protest against lockdown measures. Are we not therefore currently witnessing the relegitimization and destigmatization of conspiracy theories? And is this not due above all to the ever-growing influence of the internet?[1]

The same point was made as early as 1998 by the German media studies scholar Gundolf Freyermuth in an article subtitled 'The internet proves fertile ground for conspiracy theories', and numerous journalists and academics have since concurred with this assessment.[2] Intuitively speaking, this interpretation is indeed very convincing; after all, the internet turns the conspiracy theorist's mantra that 'everything is connected' into reality. The interpretive logic of conspiracy theories mirrors the ordering principle of the World Wide Web. A few clicks will take you from Barack Obama to the New World Order, and thence to the Ukraine crisis, thus readily creating the impression that these things are connected in reality (as opposed to mere virtual reality), and that whoever is behind the New World Order was also responsible for Obama's election as president and the unleashing of the Ukraine conflict, for example. Moreover, the internet has made it easier to question the narratives presented by the media and politicians. Information is much more readily accessible than it was in the analogue age, so that (perceived) contradictions can be exposed more promptly. Similarly, digital technology allows alternative explanations to be circulated with far greater ease and speed. There is absolutely no doubt that the internet exerts a major influence on the spread and impact of conspiracy theories. But the situation is more complicated than it appears at first sight.

It is true – as we will see in the first part of this chapter – that the internet has boosted the popularity of conspiracy theories. But this is mainly due to the greater visibility it has given them, after a long shadowy existence among subcultures on the fringes of society. Nowadays, such content is at everyone's fingertips and, as a result, it attracts more believers than two or three decades ago. This increase is by no means as substantial as one might think, however. Much more significant is the way the internet has encouraged the emergence of echo chambers and filter bubbles populated by people with similar beliefs and attitudes. In some of these sub- and counterpublics – as I demonstrate in the next section – conspiracy theories have indeed re-emerged as a perfectly acceptable form of knowledge, while in others the stigma remains. This trend has not followed the same pattern throughout the Western world, however, as a comparison between the USA and Germany shows. In the United States, the fragmentation of society is the result of a longer process that has merely been amplified by the advent of the internet. In Germany, on the other hand, that fragmentation only really began online, though its effects have long since made themselves felt in the analogue world.

Conspiracy theorists who post on the internet are therefore largely communicating with a public that either already believes, or is all too willing to believe, their allegations. In addition they use social media platforms such as Twitter and Instagram, whose specific logic imposes severe limits on length. All this has a decisive impact on the form and narrative logic of conspiracy theories. Although one still encounters expansive narratives promoting a particular theory and backing it up with copious amounts of supposed evidence, the web has now become dominated by 'texts' (in the loosest sense of the term) which either offer multiple, often contradictory conspiracist explanations side by side, or simply spread conspiracy rumours unsupported by any evidence. I discuss this change in the form of conspiracy theories in the third part of this chapter, before concluding with a case study of Donald Trump. In many respects, the forty-fifth president of the United States, a prime example of so many of the trends that I describe, provides a focal point for my reflections not just in this chapter, but in the book as a whole.

The 'truth' is just a Google search away

In the mid-1960s, Harold Weisberg was running a poultry farm in Maryland. During the Second World War he had worked for the Office of Strategic Services (the precursor of the CIA) and thereafter in Washington, DC – first in the Senate and later as a journalist – before retiring to the country. There, in the autumn of 1964, he – like many other Americans – read the recently published report by the Warren Commission following its inquiry on behalf of the US Senate into the murder of John F. Kennedy. And, like some other Americans, Weisberg was left with serious doubts as to whether Lee Harvey Oswald really had acted alone in Dallas on 22 November 1963.

Unlike most sceptics, however, Weisberg didn't stop there, but began his own investigation. A year later, he published the results in the book *Whitewash* – an independent venture, since no publisher would take it on. In it, Weisberg argued that Oswald could not have acted alone and that Kennedy had therefore been the victim of a conspiracy. In so doing, he became one of a whole series of conspiracy theorists to pick apart the Warren report over the following years. All agreed that Oswald was not a lone wolf, but disagreed over who was really behind the assassination and why it was carried out. Some blamed the CIA, others the mafia, the Cubans, the military, Kennedy's successor Lyndon B. Johnson, or all of the above. Beyond the small circle of 'assassination scholars', however, very little attention was paid to Weisberg's book, or indeed to the ten others he wrote in subsequent years, either on the same subject or on the murder of Martin Luther King Jr. in 1968.[3]

Exactly forty years after the publication of *Whitewash*, the then twenty-three-year-old Dylan Avery released the film *Loose Change* on the internet. *Loose Change* is a critical analysis of the final report by the 9/11 Commission, which was published in summer 2004. The film attempts to prove that the official version of events is false, and that the Bush administration carried out the attacks itself in order to push through its foreign and domestic policy objectives. Avery, who, according to his own story, was inspired to take on 9/11 by *The Sopranos* star James Gandolfini at a party, produced the film on a laptop for a few thousand dollars, together with his friends Korey Rowe and Jason Bermas. The three of them obtained most of the visual material from news broadcasts, created a few animations of their own, asked a friend to produce a hip-hop soundtrack and overlaid the resulting potpourri with a voiceover by Avery giving a running commentary on the content.[4]

Loose Change became a hit practically overnight. Within a year, the original film and the revised version released shortly afterwards had received several million views or downloads, prompting the magazine *Vanity Fair* to describe it as the first blockbuster of the internet age. In the period up to 2009, Avery brought out several more versions. The last one, *Loose Change: An American Coup*, presents the attacks of 9/11 as the latest chapter in a long history of US government plots against its own people. Not just 9/11, but the entire history of America since the Second World War are now cast as the result of a conspiracy. This version of the film was produced by Alex Jones at a cost of approximately 2.5 million dollars, and was narrated by the actor Daniel Sunjata, at that time one of the main characters in the popular TV series *Rescue Me*. To describe *Loose Change* as a success story is certainly no exaggeration.[5]

Whitewash and *Loose Change* may be extreme examples, but they highlight the changing status of conspiracy theories, first as a result of their delegitimization in the late 1950s, and later in response to the internet age. As discussed in the previous chapter, the stigmatization of conspiracism did not mean that people no longer produced or consumed such narratives. Even though fewer people believed in conspiracy theories in the USA and Europe from the 1960s onwards, a significant proportion of the population continued to do so. Because conspiracy theories were now stigmatized, however, they led a largely covert existence until around the turn of the millennium. Until then, the critical stance of the media and general public made it very difficult for their disseminators to reach a wider audience.

While other conspiracy theorists poring over the Kennedy assassination were not compelled to self-publish their findings like Weisberg, they too failed to achieve a broad impact. Studies arguing that belief in conspiracy theories has steadily increased in recent decades invariably point to opinion polls which they claim show that since the mid-1960s at least a third of Americans have harboured doubts about the official version of events at any one time. But this argument – as Katharina Thalmann has convincingly demonstrated – is wrong. Rather than a steady increase, these regular surveys actually show a great deal of fluctuation. Directly after the assassination, for example, more than 60 per cent of respondents believed in a conspiracy; after the publication of the Warren Commission report, however, that number fell to 31 per cent. The following decades saw similar variations, again mostly due to new official investigations rather than the texts of 'assassination scholars', which generally failed to achieve a high circulation and were not prominently placed in bookshops or positively reviewed in newspapers.[6] Aware of the stigma attached to their ideas, some of these scholars did not even try to reach the sceptical public. Instead, they

shared their findings within a fairly close circle, via phone
calls, private letters, annual conferences or magazines such
as *Minority of One*, which specialized in conspiracy theories
and whose very title is an attempt to turn their stigma into
a mark of moral superiority. This conspiracist subculture
barely impinged on the public consciousness, however.[7]

Consequently, anyone entertaining only vague doubts
about the official version of the Kennedy assassination
was unlikely to come into contact with the speculations of
die-hard conspiracy theorists, whether perusing the morning
papers, browsing their favourite bookshop in the lunch
break, or watching TV at night. Being out of favour,
conspiracy theorists usually didn't make it into the media,
and if they did, their ideas were invariably framed in
sarcastic or alarmist language. They were either ridiculed or
– on the strength of Richard Hofstadter's widely acclaimed
essay, which was first published a year before *Whitewash*
– identified as bordering on clinical paranoia, a fact which
is bound to have deterred many other doubters. In short,
anyone in the 1970s and 1980s even contemplating the
possibility that Oswald did not act alone had their work
cut out to obtain confirmation for this idea. Finding full-
fledged conspiracy theories required active searching, and the
investment of time and money. This was hard enough in the
USA, but harder still elsewhere. Some of the American texts,
but far from all, were translated into German. Nor was there
– either in Germany or elsewhere – a network of Kennedy
conspiracy theorists.

As a result, many of those on either side of the Atlantic
who would otherwise have been quite receptive to conspiracist explanations are highly unlikely to have seen their
vague doubts harden into full-blown conspiracy theories.
Even Oliver Stone's 1991 film *JFK* – which made 200 million
dollars worldwide, won two Oscars and was nominated for
eight – did nothing to change this. Although it did spark a
resurgence of mistrust in the official story which was duly
reflected in opinion polls, this was short-lived and soon
died down again – no doubt partly due to the film's highly
critical reception in the media, despite the great admiration
for Stone's technical skill. Besides, the film only shone a
brief light on one particular conspiracy theory, while others

– whether about the moon landing, Watergate or the New World Order – remained entirely below the public radar.

With the internet, all that changed. Whereas readers' letters promoting conspiracy theories were once filtered out by editors keen to spare their readership what they deemed to be nonsense, anyone can now leave a comment below an article on a reputable website in a matter of seconds, adding a link to websites and blogs that actively disseminate conspiracist narratives. While it takes a substantial amount of time and money to self-publish a book like Harold Weisberg's, websites and social networking profiles are easy to set up and virtually cost-free. And while it used to be almost impossible for an amateur to make a feature-length documentary that was half-way professional in terms of editing, soundtrack and other formal elements, digital technology has made this task a whole lot easier too, as the example of *Loose Change* shows.

As for those seeking conspiracist alternatives, the internet has been similarly transformative. Nowadays, such content can be found without investing the least money or effort; on the contrary, anyone with the slightest inclination to inform themselves and perhaps even question what they hear in the media can hardly escape it online. The traditional watchdog role of the media has been largely nullified by the possibilities of the World Wide Web; in the digital age, the 'truth' is always just a Google search away.

A small experiment will suffice to illustrate this. On 18 April 2019, I Googled the following 'results' in a matter of seconds – on someone else's computer in this case, as the personalized algorithms on my own laptop and office computer would obviously short-cut to the relevant sites. My search for '9/11' soon threw up the site 'http://www.911-archiv.net/', where the official version of the September 11 attacks is 'exposed' as a lie in a series of articles. Though not on the first page, it came right at the top of the second. The fact that this site – run by a German conspiracy theorist who wrote to me several times nearly ten years ago – should appear so high up in the rankings is astonishing given that it was last updated in 2015. As for the question 'Who killed Kennedy?', this produced several conspiracist accounts on the very first page, including an article entitled 'LBJ Knew

Who Killed JFK', whose author claims that documents published in summer 2018 have finally solved the riddle and confirmed the conspiracy theories. And when I entered the (admittedly loaded) words 'Ukraine regime change', I found a link – again on the very first page – to the article 'Washington Follows Ukraine, Syria Roadmap in Push for Venezuela Regime Change', which argues that the CIA orchestrated the 2014 riots in Ukraine in order to bring a pro-American government to power, and is now doing the same in Venezuela.[8]

In this way, the internet brings to public attention ideas that would have found little or no audience in the past. Orthodox and heterodox knowledge are equally accessible, and they are often presented side by side, which suggests that they are of equal value. There is no longer an editor to decide whether a given opinion is too outlandish to be published. The importance of expertise has rapidly diminished, while lay knowledge or alternative and self-appointed experts are on the rise. This levelling of knowledge hierarchies is not problematic in itself, as we can see from projects such as Wikipedia, whose English and German-language articles are of extremely high quality in many fields, as well as being more up to date than a traditional encyclopaedia. Wikipedia differs from other websites, however, in that it has quality-control measures in place, such as an arbitration committee for settling disputes. This is not the case in other areas of the internet, where we may encounter bodies of knowledge that are at odds with the current scientific wisdom, but which are often presented as scientific or superior to traditional knowledge.[9]

Naturally this has consequences. Given the constant avail-ability of all kinds of conspiracy theories, doubters in search of alternative explanations are much more likely than they were in the age of print to absorb some of the content they consume – or, as conspiracy theorists like to put it, to wake up and smell the coffee. I therefore disagree with political scientist Joe Uscinski and his colleagues who have recently argued that the internet has little or no influence on conspiracy belief because conspiracy theories on the internet '[are] only reaching and convincing those who already agree with those ideas'. The theories also reach not only those who are not (yet) absolute believers but also those who have so far merely harboured doubts.[10]

If the internet has brought about a moderate rise in the number of conspiracy believers, however, then that is also down to the new ease of networking with likeminded people. Before the internet came along, conspiracy theorists had very limited opportunities to communicate as a group. They could get in touch with each other by phone or letter, but they only came together as a community once or twice a year at most – and then only if they could afford the time and money to attend the relevant conferences, which were held almost exclusively in the USA. Nowadays, they can remain in constant contact with each other as an online group, regardless of national boundaries. That the existence of such virtual communities tends to weaken the influence of the real environment is only logical. Thirty years ago, if you were the only believer in a given conspiracy theory in your neighbourhood, you would probably have been more easily talked out of it by those around you than today, when you can go online and find confirmation for your ideas.

Accordingly, the internet has given a new boost to conspiracy theories. But that increase is not as great as is often claimed. When polls indicate that half of all Americans believe in at least one conspiracy theory, that may sound like a large number on the face of it, especially to someone who knows nothing of the history of conspiracy theories. But even thirty years ago, there was always a certain constituency who believed the Kennedy assassination to be a coup d'état and the moon landing a staged TV stunt. And, as we saw in the previous chapter, conspiracy theories were even more popular in the preceding centuries. If Eric Oliver and Thomas Wood had interviewed people in 1814 or 1914, the number of conspiracy believers would have been much higher than that recorded in their major study of 2014. By comparison with the long period up to 1960 when conspiracy theories constituted a perfectly legitimate form of knowledge, they are still languishing in obscurity. That they have regained any popularity at all over the last few years is due to the media conditions of the internet rather than humanity becoming more stupid. The impression that such theories have suddenly become omnipresent – an alarming one for many – is false. It only holds true for certain sections of society; in others, now as before, it is not belief in, but concern about conspiracy theories that predominates.[11]

Relegitimization in the echo chamber

There has been much discussion over the past few years of the trend towards 'echo chambers' and 'filter bubbles', meaning that our online experience confronts us almost exclusively (unless we go out of our way to avoid it) with information that reinforces our existing assumptions. The algorithms of the search engines and social media we use ensure that the results pages of our searches and the newsfeeds of our social networking profiles only feature content that confirms what we already believe. This trend is especially pronounced among followers of conspiracy theories, as the mathematician Michela Del Vicario and her team recently demonstrated in a large-scale empirical study. Conspiracy believers tend to inhabit and communicate within clearly delimited online communities.[12]

That they are able to do so is due to the emergence of a plethora of alternative media claiming to counter the allegedly biased and sometimes even deliberately manipulated information presented by the traditional media with the voice of truth. These include websites such as breitbart.com or infowars.com in the USA and klagemauer.tv or compact-online.de in the German-speaking countries. In addition, there are countless YouTube channels entirely devoted to the popularization of conspiracist ideas. Browsing through the comments below the video of a talk by David Ray Griffin, one of the leading figures in the 9/11 Truth Movement, or a report by Alex Jones's team, it is difficult to find a critical voice. On the contrary, the users confirm each other in the view that someone is finally speaking the truth.

The effect of such echo chambers is a fragmentation of the public sphere. The internet has given rise to counter-publics which, as we shall see in a moment, are interwoven in multiple ways with the real world, and where conspiracy theories are once again considered legitimate knowledge. Members of these publics may reject the label 'conspiracy theorist' (or perhaps sport it with pride), but they do not question the basic assumptions of the conspiracist rationale. They may differ on the details (what exactly caused the Twin Towers of the World Trade Center to collapse?) or disagree over who precisely was operating behind the scenes (the Bush administration? The New World Order?), but they all agree on the existence of large-scale conspiracies (the official version of 9/11 is a lie). At the same time, there are other publics where conspiracy theories are still stigmatized as illegitimate knowledge – the academic community, for example, or what conspiracy theorists contemptuously refer to as the 'mainstream media' or the *Lügenpresse*, the 'lying press'.

This phenomenon is, of course, not new. Multiple publics also existed back in the age of the classic Habermasian 'bourgeois public sphere', and not all of them subscribed to the same concept of truth. But it is a recent development that conspiracy theories have spawned counterpublics with their own media systems and experts that are easily locatable, accessible or at least observable as such from the outside; up to then, conspiracy theories were confined to fairly hermetic subcultures – like the John Birch Society in the USA, or ufologists all over the world. And even when some of these subcultures evolved into counterpublics, the hierarchy between them was generally much clearer back then than it is today. Although we have not yet reached a stage of absolute parity between these parts of the public where conspiracy theories are (once again) perfectly acceptable and those where they are (still) taboo, the hierarchy has nevertheless begun to shift. Accordingly, the articulation of conspiracy theories is now often judged less harshly even in Western societies than was the case a few years ago.

To take three examples: Michael Flynn Jr. was sacked from Donald Trump's transition team for stoking the 'Pizzagate' conspiracy theory on Twitter, which claimed that members of Hillary Clinton's election campaign team were operating a child pornography ring behind the facade of a Washington pizzeria. Despite this, Michael Flynn Sr., who had also been spreading his son's tweets, was appointed Trump's National Security Advisor, although he was soon forced to resign over the Russian affair. In Germany, the MP Wolfgang Gedeon had to leave the Alternative for Germany group in the Baden-Württemberg state parliament over his anti-Semitic conspiracy theories, but did not lose his seat. Finally, writing in the *Daily Telegraph*, once firmly situated within the part of the public that considered conspiracy theories illegitimate knowledge, Allison Pearson alleged in November 2018 that Theresa May and other members of the government were actively sabotaging Brexit: 'Signs of the Conspiracy against Brexit are everywhere', she claimed.[13]

As these examples show, the same tendency is observable in several countries. That said, the fragmentation of the public sphere is not equally advanced in all cases. The interaction between the digital and analogue world also varies from country to country, as a comparison between the USA and Germany shows. I will leave aside the UK here, as this is the most complicated case and would exceed the scope of this section. In my view, however, it sits somewhere between the two, having a political system resembling that of the USA in that it is dominated by two parties due to a first-past-the-post voting system, and a media system similar to Germany's in that it has strong public service broadcasters that are not driven primarily by commercial interests.

In the United States, the disintegration of the public sphere into echo chambers began long before the arrival of the internet, which has merely accelerated and amplified the process. As the political scientist Torben Lütjen has shown, the fragmentation of US society can be traced back to the mid-twentieth century. Up to then, although only two parties had seriously competed for power for over a hundred years, there was no question of any polarization of the political system, as the Democrats and Republicans were virtually indistinguishable in terms of ideology. Dwight D. Eisenhower, who won the 1952 presidential election for the Republicans, had also been wooed by the Democrats and had seriously considered running on their ticket. That this would be unthinkable today is a reflection of how far the parties have drifted apart since the 1960s. While the Democrats have become increasingly liberal, the Republicans have grown progressively more conservative.[14]

The specifics of the party political landscape are just one factor in this fragmentation process, however. Another is the break-up of the media landscape that followed in the wake of the parties' divergence and began once the political radicalization was largely complete. During the so-called network era from around 1950 to the late 1980s, the US television market was dominated by the three major broadcasting corporations ABC, NBC and CBS and their affiliated local stations. Their coverage tended to be very similar, and aspired to objectivity and neutrality. With the advent of cable TV and the transformation of the radio environment, all that changed. Although the big networks still exist, their influence has greatly diminished and, apart from the broadcaster PBS, there is no equivalent to the British or German public service media. Instead, the media scene is dominated by countless TV and radio stations seeking to promote a very specific world view. The right-wing conservative channel Fox News, which continues to give Donald Trump an extremely favourable press, is the most well-known example of this, and now actually constitutes one of the more moderate voices if we compare its coverage with that of sites such as breitbart.com.[15]

This is not to say, however, that the fragmentation of the US public along political lines corresponds to the divide between those who believe in conspiracy theories and those who don't. Rather, what we are dealing with here are multiple fragmentations of the public sphere. American society is as firmly divided between supporters of the two big parties – and a considerable number of undecideds in the middle – as it is divided between those who worry about conspiracies and those who worry about conspiracy theories. These divides – alongside others not relevant to our discussion here – partly overlap and partly do not. After all, if one is convinced that one's own party is the only reasonable choice in an election, the only viable alternative for the good of the country, one might be inclined to think that something sinister must be going on if the other party succeeds. This explains why conspiracy theories arose among Democrats after the defeat of Hillary Clinton and why so many of those who abhor Trump were disappointed when the Mueller report did not find conclusive evidence for collusion or conspiracy with Russia.[16]

In Germany, by contrast, the fragmentation of the public sphere only began in earnest with the possibilities opened up by the internet. Because there are more parties in Germany, because they are in many respects not so far apart ideologically as the USA's Democrats and Republicans, and because the proportional voting system constantly compels them to enter into coalitions with each other, the split between the virtual and real environment is less advanced there than in the USA. As a comprehensive data search conducted by the newspaper *Süddeutsche Zeitung* on the main parties' Facebook pages in the months leading up to the 2017 Bundestag election showed, there is (as yet) no real evidence of filter bubbles, in the sense of a closed circle impervious to outside influence. Indeed, one can hardly even speak of echo chambers as far as the established parties are concerned, since most of the posts on their sites refer to the same mainstream news sources. One exception, however, is that of supporters of the Alternative for Germany party, whose exchanges positively do take place in an echo chamber. Tellingly, conspiracy theories are far more widespread among followers and representatives of this party than any other, and flourish in the closed online forums and Facebook groups used by their community.[17]

Even in Germany, however, conspiracy theorists no longer have to rely on the internet alone for 'alternative' news sources confirming them in their beliefs. Whereas, in the USA, the advent of the digital age has amplified conditions already prevailing in the analogue media, the opposite trend is observable in Germany. The clearest illustration of this is the emergence, respectively, of the magazine *Compact* and the publisher Kopp Verlag, the two biggest producers of conspiracy theories in the German print media industry. *Compact*, whose editorial office is based in Leipzig, has been published on a monthly basis since 2010 and currently sells around 40,000 copies of each issue. Its editor-in-chief and figurehead since 2013 is the journalist Jürgen Elsässer, who used to write for more left-leaning publications before breaking with these and becoming an opinion leader of the New Right. *Compact*, whose strapline 'Magazine for Sovereignty' already suggests its predilection for conspiracy theories that see the Federal Republic as being undermined by dark forces and robbed of its independence, is available at many kiosks. The magazine's rapid rise would scarcely have been possible without its strong online presence, however.

New articles continue to appear daily on compact-online. de, whose purpose is of course to recruit new readers for the print edition. The same function is performed by the magazine's YouTube channel, where each new issue is advertised with brief reports and a discussion panel, and also by its Facebook page, where the print titles are announced, some articles are published exclusively, and readers can join the discussion.

Kopp Verlag, which is based in Rottenburg, near Tübingen, was founded in 1994 by the ex-policeman Jochen Kopp. Alongside esoteric texts, it specializes in conspiracist and right-wing populist literature, as well as survival kits, vitamins and personal care products. The product range is very similar to that of Alex Jones's online store. Kopp-Verlag was long confined to a niche existence, but has since gained enormously in popularity and seen its sales soar over the past few years thanks to its internet presence, and of course to the surge in right-wing populism. According to its owner, it sold 'between 10,000 and 25,000 books a day' in 2015. The books continue to be sold directly on the internet, rather than indirectly through booksellers.[18]

Far from being mere fringe phenomena, *Compact* and the output of Kopp Verlag command a substantial public. Indeed, at the Württemberg state library, where Kopp is obliged to deposit copies of all its publications, the books are among the most commonly requested and reserved items in the contemporary history department.[19] That said, neither conspiracy belief nor the fragmentation of the public is as far advanced in Germany as it is in the USA. While statistical surveys on conspiracy belief are – as discussed in Chapter 3 – not unproblematic, the only sizeable studies conducted in Germany show that theories of this kind are still less popular there than in the USA.[20]

This has an impact on the rhetoric of those who (whether they believe in it themselves or not) seek to derive political capital from conspiracism. Representatives of the AfD generally avoid being too up-front about conspiracy theories in public. At most, they send out ambivalent signals which can, but need not necessarily, be understood in a conspiracist sense. The manifesto statement quoted in the previous chapter claiming that sovereignty over the country actually lies with 'a small, powerful political elite within the parties' is a good example of this. When AfD members are amongst their own, the tone is often very different. Although it was never conclusively established whether the email published by *Die Welt* shortly before the election – in which the members of the Merkel administration were branded 'puppets of the victorious powers of World War II' – really did come from Alice Weidel, chairwoman of the AfD in the Bundestag, it would be consistent with a party whose leadership is (so far) much less inclined to take a conspiracist line in its external than in its internal communications.[21]

This may not remain the case, however, as a further comparison with the USA shows. In a conversation in 2009 with supporters who doubted the legitimacy of Barack Obama's election – because they believed that he was not born in the USA and that his birth certificate was falsified – the vice-presidential candidate Sarah Palin said that 'The public rightfully is still making it an issue', and that 'The McCain-Palin campaign didn't do a good enough job in that area.' When Palin's statements were picked up by the media, however, she quickly backpedalled, announcing on Facebook that she had merely meant to say that voters were entitled to ask any question they liked. She and others were happy to share the reservations of the so-called birthers as long as there were no cameras running. A year later, congressman Ken Buck from Kansas told his staff point blank: 'Tell those dumbasses at the Tea Party to stop asking questions about birth certificates while I'm on camera.' At that time, then, Republican candidates still exercised restraint in public, presumably in order to avoid scaring off more moderate voters. Eight years on, however, their party's presidential candidate showed no such restraint.[22]

From conspiracy theories to conspiracy rumours

The so-called birther conspiracy theory is a good example of how conspiracist discourse has changed as a result of the internet. In August 2016, Katharina Thalmann and I taught a two-week seminar on conspiracy theories at a summer academy run by the German Academic Scholarship Foundation. After an initial plenary session where we outlined the basic concepts, the students were asked to research various conspiracy theories in small groups. This worked well for 9/11 or the refugee crisis, for which the students found a wealth of conspiracist texts, but not at all for the birther conspiracy theory. Despite encountering plenty of tweets claiming that Barack Obama was born outside the USA and videos appearing to prove that his birth certificate was faked, the students failed to find any texts or videos explaining who was behind the plot and what its purpose was. Nowhere were allegedly classified documents picked apart, or the motives of supposed miscreants inferred from apparently harmless actions and statements. There is no end of material explicitly claiming or implicitly suggesting a conspiracy, but I do not know of a single source that attempts to prove this in the usual manner of conspiracy theories. As such, the birthers' allegations do not amount to a conspiracy theory, but rather a conspiracy rumour.

The claims regarding Obama's birthplace (usually alleged to be Kenya) were among the first conspiracist ideas to be spread in this form. Nowadays, many of the conspiracy theories circulated online are more rumours than fully fledged theories. As such, they are the latest stage of a three-phase development. Not that the older forms disappear altogether, they simply become less important compared to the newer forms. Thus, in the case of the refugee crisis, an online search yields both conspiracy rumours and 'old-fashioned' conspiracy theories purporting to reveal the masterminds and their plots.

This development began before the internet proper became popular, namely in the late 1980s with a global electronic network called Usenet which still exists today and which allows its users to share information on a variety of topics in so-called newsgroups. These newsgroups operate like discussion forums on the web, except that only text posts are possible and, in the early days especially, communication was much slower than in the World Wide Web, as many users would download the posts first in order to read and answer them offline before finally uploading their own comments. Conspiracy theorists were quick to catch on to both Usenet and the early internet forums, as these channels allowed the kind of information sharing denied to them by the traditional media.

In the early 1990s in particular, such forms of virtual exchange were occasionally used by conspiracy theorists in order to develop collective conspiracy narratives and pool evidence. Since much of the content from this time is no longer accessible, it is difficult to reconstruct it, so an example will have to suffice – namely the debate surrounding the alleged murder of the journalist Danny Casolaro, which Mark Fenster has analysed in detail. Many conspiracy theorists refused to believe that Casolaro (mentioned briefly back in Chapter 2) committed suicide in August 1991, regarding him instead as the victim of a major conspiracy he was said to have uncovered. From spring 1992 onwards, they exploited the possibilities of the internet and Usenet quite deliberately in order to piece together the puzzle and prevent important information from being lost. The result, while failing to present an entirely coherent overall picture, was nevertheless a superconspiracy theory, whose various versions linked Casolaro's death to events as disparate as the Iran-Contra affair or the Kennedy assassination. Fenster therefore rightly describes the content constructed via these virtual platforms as a 'collective true crime story'.[23]

There are limits to this collective practice, however, because conspiracy theorists tend to view not just those in power, but also those around them with suspicion. This may be prompted by the at least potentially conceivable possibility that opponents will try to sabotage their community. Or it may be born of sheer jealousy towards those whose posts are more popular, or the impossibility of agreeing on a single explanation. The main purpose of forums and newsgroups was and is, therefore, to allow users to share information without obligation, reinforce their mutual belief in the falsity of the official version, and point to sources of interest in the virtual or real world. Another form of such collective action is the expression of gratitude to and admiration for those whose conspiracy narratives have achieved a large following within the community. Nowadays, this mainly takes the form of comments under videos of talks by celebrities such as David Icke and feature-length documentaries such as the

Loose Change series, whose appearance around 2005 marks the beginning of the next phase in the development discussed here.[24]

Around this time, more and more conspiracy theorists – motivated chiefly by the September 11 attacks and what they saw as an unsatisfactory report by the 9/11 Commission – began to exploit the possibilities of digital and internet technology in order to produce documentaries attempting to prove a conspiracy. As already mentioned in Chapter 2, these films are a collage of all kinds of visual material, from news clips through interviews to animated sequences. Hardly any of these images were produced by the conspiracy theorists themselves; instead, they were assembled from countless sources, arranged in a particular order and provided with a soundtrack and voiceover interpreting the visual content for the viewer and articulating the conspiracy theory underlying the whole thing.

Besides *Loose Change*, the best-known conspiracist films dating from this phase are the second and third parts of the *Zeitgeist* trilogy by Peter Joseph, which were first released in 2007. Like *Loose Change*, the second part attributes responsibility for 9/11 to the US government, while the third claims that both world wars and the Vietnam conflict were staged by a group of international bankers. Again like *Loose Change*, the *Zeitgeist* films were initially available via Google Video, but were soon also released on YouTube, where the most popular one was a specially produced version of the third part focusing on the Federal Reserve, the USA's central bank, and its role in a number of alleged plots. In terms of aesthetics, this version is even closer to the *Loose Change* films than the original ones. The opening sequence in particular, in which a series of portentous quotes ranging from the eighteenth century to the present appear in white lettering on a black background, echoes the second version of *Loose Change*, which uses the same technique to link the 1960s with the year 2001.[25]

As with the *Loose Change* films, there are also various versions of the *Zeitgeist* films – in fact Joseph updated and re-released the entire trilogy in 2010. This constant process of revision is typical of conspiracist internet films from the first decade of the twenty-first century. Thanks to digital technology, such updates have become much easier to perform. Sequences can be copied from the old version to the new one, graphics and special effects can be optimized with the aid of ever more sophisticated software, and individual images can be swapped in an instant. In this sense, the technical possibilities play into the conspiracist logic, particularly in an age of stigmatization. After all, as we saw in earlier chapters, the interpretative task of the conspiracy theorist is never really complete: there is always more evidence to discover and new developments to integrate into the narrative. It is therefore fitting that *Loose Change Final Cut* did not remain the last film of the series, and that Avery and his team went on to produce the version *An American Coup* a few years later. For conspiracy theorists, there is never a definitive last word. Moreover, this willingness to go on revising allows the producers to present themselves as open to criticism, in contrast to the stereotypical conspiracy theorist who refuses to accept even the most convincing arguments. Such openness is, however, an illusion. If we compare the various versions of *Loose Change* and *Zeitgeist*, we soon realize that nothing has changed in terms of the actual thrust of the argument or the overarching narrative. The conspirators of the first version are still the bad guys in the last one. Only minor details in the argument have been changed.

The last internet versions of *Loose Change* and *Zeitgeist* appeared in 2009 and 2010. The reason that no more have been made since is not that the producers have lost interest in conspiracy theories, but rather that the format has to some extent been exhausted. Although lengthy online documentaries are still produced, they no longer command anything like the audiences achieved by Avery, Joseph or even Alex Jones (with *The Obama Deception* of 2009). These 'classics' from the first decade of this century are of course still available online, and continue to be viewed – as is clear from the dates of the comments below the films – but not nearly as intensively as in the years when they were made. This is largely because other formats have taken the place of documentaries as the most important medium for conspiracist ideas. No one dominant form is currently discernible, however, but rather a range of different approaches that are equally popular.

One approach much in vogue at the moment is to film talks by high-profile conspiracy theorists before a live audience and post them on YouTube. The same goes for interviews with these stars of the alternative media, which are much more prolific today than they were ten years ago. Enter 'Daniele Ganser' or 'David Ray Griffin' in the YouTube search engine for example, and you will be inundated with hits. To date, Ganser's most popular talks have received more than a million clicks and thousands of comments. Although these figures are not quite on a par with Griffin's, his talks are watched on average by tens of thousands of people. Thanks to YouTube, therefore, the top conspiracy theorists are now able to reach a sizeable audience. At the same time, we are witnessing an increasing coalescence between the virtual and real world within the context of conspiracist counterpublics. What began just under twenty years ago on the internet is now having an impact well beyond it. Today, conspiracy theories are filling not just virtual spaces, but whole lecture theatres.

In the vast majority of cases, the talks available on YouTube are still dominated by one particular narrative or conspiracy theory for which alleged evidence is advanced. The same is true of live social media feeds, which conspiracy theorists are now increasingly generating on unfolding events and integrating into an existing conspiracy narrative. When Notre Dame cathedral went up in flames on the evening of 15 April 2019, for example, the German conspiracy theorist Bodo Schickentanz popped up live on Facebook, declaring the disaster another 'Reichstag fire'. His assumptions were based – in classic conspiracist style – on the 'cui bono?' principle. In this instance, he argued, the beneficiary was Macron, whom he had been accusing for months of using brutal violence against the yellow vest protesters, allegedly because their agenda conflicted with the interests of his own supporters. According to Schickentanz, the fire saved Macron from having to respond to the yellow vests' demands in his long-awaited TV address.[26]

By contrast, another online format that has seen an upsurge in recent years, namely the conspiracist blog, has largely moved away from the concept of a dominant narrative. The very nature of the blog medium, i.e. its episodic seriality, means that conflicting conspiracist tropes are often directly juxtaposed. Blogs of this kind can be divided into two main types. Firstly, there are those like globalresearch.ca, which draw simultaneously on virtually every conspiracy theory going, jumping between articles on 9/11, the Skripal affair, the Notre Dame fire and other alleged plots. And secondly, there are those that concentrate on a single topic, be it 9/11 or refugees. In both cases, however, mutually contradictory memes from different conspiracy narratives are simply placed side by side. Rarely is there any attempt to integrate them into a coherent narrative.

Besides the constraints of the medium, another reason for such indeterminacy is that these blogs are aimed at readers who are already critical of state institutions and the truths they 'sell'. Unlike evening-filling documentaries such as *Loose Change*, their purpose is no longer to convince neutral or even averse readers of the existence of a conspiracy. Their target audience is one that either already believes in conspiracy theories or is at least inclined to do so, having actively searched for counter-narratives. Since the object is to reach as many readers as possible and cover the maximum number of topics of interest to them, it would hardly be practicable – in fact it would be more of a hindrance – to weigh up different conspiracist explanations, corroborating some while criticizing others. In that case, not all readers would feel confirmed in their beliefs.[27]

Even vaguer is a new type of internet video that has likewise emerged in the last few years. It consists of brief clips – often just a few minutes long – posted in response to day-to-day events. That way, conspiracy theorists can exploit the possibilities of social media networks such as YouTube or Facebook in order to comment on the latest developments far more quickly than they could in conventional media formats. The makers of these clips either speak direct to camera or use a voiceover to comment on images taken from news broadcasts or other sources. After the devastating attack of October 2017 in Las Vegas, in which fifty-eight people were killed, videos started appearing within hours on YouTube attempting to prove, through pictures of the attack, survivors' statements and 'mainstream media' coverage, that the massacre either never happened or was orchestrated by the state. Characteristically, nearly all the videos offer up both possibilities without committing to one side or the other. The only thing the makers are clear about is that the official version is false.[28]

The video by 'Agent S' about Hillary Clinton which I analysed in Chapter 2 also belongs to this new genre. What I didn't mention back then is that the maker does not integrate Clinton's supposed replacement by a double into a specific conspiracy theory, but changes the subject towards the end of the video in order to speculate whether she might be dead (he is unable to decide whether she died on that day or long before). What we are dealing with here is no longer a conspiracy theory in the classical sense. While Agent S starts out by using the familiar mechanisms of conspiracist argumentation in order to interpret the images on the screen, the resulting insights do not form a piece of the overall puzzle; instead, he turns immediately to other ideas that have no bearing on what he has just been at pains to demonstrate. The upshot is not a conspiracy theory, but a conglomeration of conspiracy rumours.[29]

This equivocality is no doubt motivated by the desire to attract the largest possible audience. The videos target different groups by offering something for everyone: those who are convinced that Hillary Clinton was replaced by a body double on 11 September 2016 due to pneumonia; those who believe that she was already long dead and that this had therefore been going on for some time; and those who think it possible that she died on that precise day. There are most likely commercial interests behind this strategy. By picking up on as many of the currently circulating rumours as possible, conspiracy theorists like Agent S can pepper their videos with all the latest buzzwords and so attract more viewers, which in turn boosts their advertising revenue. Here, then, is an instance of how the increasing commercialization of conspiracist discourse is driving the trend towards conspiracy rumours.

Another factor fuelling this trend is the ever-growing popularity of the microblogging service Twitter. While it is at least theoretically possible to post longer, more complex texts in blogs and on Facebook and hence to develop full-blown conspiracy theories, Twitter limited individual posts initially to 140 characters and, from autumn 2017, to 280 – that's fewer than in this sentence. Although one could conceivably develop a more elaborate conspiracy narrative in a series of tweets – a so-called thread – this is practically never done, as it runs counter to the logic of the medium. What Twitter calls for, by contrast, are brief soundbites and unsubstantiated claims – in short, rumours. In fact, tweets no longer even need to be backed up with evidence, as the emerging echo chambers ensure that they are most likely to reach those who are already predisposed to believe the sender. For this reason, Twitter is the ideal medium for mobilizing followers, whether in relation to a conspiracy rumour or anything else. And of all Western politicians, no one has grasped this as well as Donald Trump.

Case study: Donald Trump

It is surely no exaggeration to say that, without Barack Obama and Twitter, Donald Trump would never have ended up in the White House. Whole swathes of the electorate who voted for Trump did so because they rejected everything the first black president and Hillary Clinton, who would have been the first female president, stood for. And it was through Twitter that Trump first became politically active in the loosest sense of the word – characteristically, by seizing on the conspiracy rumour that Obama was not born in the USA (and should not therefore have been allowed to become president). From autumn 2011, but especially in spring 2012, Trump made allegations to this effect in a whole series of tweets and went on to repeat them in interviews whenever the matter was raised by journalists. 'Made in America? Barack Obama called his "birthplace" Hawaii "here in Asia"', one tweet of 18 November 2011 exclaimed, for example. According to observers – and this assessment is confirmed by sources close to Trump – these allegations, popular among disillusioned conservatives, gave Trump a welcome opportunity to build on his image as a businessman and TV star and establish himself in the political arena as a spokesman for concerned citizens. Whether Trump really believed that Obama was not eligible to be president is something only he knows; the point is, his tweets proved an effective way of accumulating political capital. Having road-tested this strategy, he then dropped it again in order to bide his time. The 2012 election came too early for him; at that stage, he would not have stood a chance against the widely popular Obama.[30]

Less than four years later, the strategic deployment of conspiracy rumours and theories became a hallmark of Trump's campaign to succeed Obama. Initially ridiculed by the press and his rivals following the official announcement of his candidacy in July 2015, he soon rose to become the favourite for the Republican nomination, then went on to win it, and eventually to defeat Hillary Clinton, having secured a majority in the decisive electoral college, though not the majority of the popular vote. The surprising part of this – at least at first sight – was Trump's increasing use of conspiracist rhetoric the closer it got to the November 2016 election. Normally, candidates in the United States have to adopt radical positions during the primaries in order to beat their party-internal rivals, but tend to soften their tone when it comes to the election campaign itself. If we consider Trump's campaign more closely, however, his course of action is perfectly logical. From the outset, Trump presented himself as the anti-establishment candidate, and conspiracy rumours helped him to articulate this position. At first, he stuck to rumours to avoid scaring off moderate voters, but once it became clear that he wasn't scoring highly enough with this group, he began to formulate detailed conspiracy theories in order to mobilize his core voters, many of whom hadn't voted in the previous elections.

Throughout the almost year-long primaries within the Republican Party and the five months of the election campaign proper, Trump drew on an array of conspiracy theories: that vaccinations cause autism; that climate change was invented by foreign powers in order to damage the American economy; that Trump's rival Ted Cruz was born in Canada and was therefore not eligible to stand; that Cruz's father met with Lee Harvey Oswald shortly before Oswald assassinated Kennedy; that Antonin Scalia, a Supreme Court judge who died unexpectedly in February 2016, was murdered; and that Vince Foster, who worked in the White House during Bill Clinton's presidency, was also murdered because he knew too much about the Clintons' machinations. For Trump, these

claims generally served two functions: firstly, to discredit
political opponents like Cruz or Clinton and, secondly, to
present himself (however paradoxical it may sound to those
who regard conspiracy theories as humbug) as a decent,
honest guy, a true representative of the people who – despite,
or precisely because of, its stigmatization – embraces the
conspiracist discourse frowned upon by the elites.[31]

Characteristically, however, Trump almost always left
himself a loophole in order to distance himself if necessary
from any accusation that he was spreading conspiracy
theories. As noted in Chapter 1, the claim that vaccinations
cause autism is not in itself a conspiracy theory, whereas
the claim that such risks are being covered up, or that the
underlying intention is to cause autism, are. And that is
precisely what Trump avoided doing. In his speeches, he
also invariably prefaced conspiracist tropes with expressions
such as 'I often hear it said that ...' or 'People tell me that
...'. In the case of the allegations against Cruz, he used the
time-honoured conspiracist device of the rhetorical question:
'What was he doing with Lee Harvey Oswald shortly before
the death of ... the shooting [of Kennedy]?'[32]

This technique of referencing conspiracy theories without
actually embracing them is most apparent in the conversation
with Alex Jones alluded to earlier. During this half-hour
interview, in which the candidate participated by satellite
from Trump Tower, New York, Jones repeatedly tries to
get Trump to comment on the major New World Order
conspiracy by putting words in his mouth. For his part,
Trump uses the opportunity to get Jones to corroborate his
own claim that New Jersey Muslims cheered the collapse of
the World Trade Center on 11 September 2001, while also
indulging at length in a populist critique of elites and the
system, but he refrains from engaging with Jones's explicitly
conspiracist claims. Nor does he need to: he is signalling by
his very participation in the programme that he takes Jones
and, by extension, conspiracy theories in general, perfectly
seriously. At the same time, his approach is designed to avoid
alienating potential voters who are sceptical of conspiracist
ideology.

Trump did not abandon this 'restraint' until a few weeks
before the election. By October 2016, he knew he had the

backing of the vast majority of traditional Republican voters. These were people who would vote for him – even if they had to hold their noses to do so – purely to prevent Hillary Clinton from becoming president. At this stage he was still behind Clinton in the polls, but within touching distance. His chances of bringing moderate, centre-ground voters on side as well and thus winning the election fell to virtually zero on 8 October however, when an audiotape was released which captured him boasting of his sexual assaults. From then on, it became more important than ever to mobilize those whose fear of economic and/or cultural marginalization made them receptive to his populist and conspiracist rhetoric, and to make sure they actually cast their vote. It is therefore anything but coincidence that Trump's appearance at the hustings in West Palm Beach, Florida on 13 October not only saw him dismiss the allegations of sexist remarks and behaviour, but also marked a transition in his approach from conspiracy rumours to conspiracy theories.

During his roughly fifty-minute-long address, Trump uses every trick of populist conspiracy rhetoric described in Chapter 4. In a departure from his campaign thus far, he makes open accusations and even claims to provide evidence. He begins by setting up the familiar opposition between the 'American people' and a 'totally corrupt ... political establishment' that exploits the people and seeks only to enrich itself. At the same time, he insists that this elite is not a purely American problem: 'It's a global power structure that is responsible for the economic decisions that have robbed our working class, stripped our country of its wealth and put that money into the pockets of a handful of large corporations and political entities.' With typical conspiracist hyperbole, Trump suggests that it is five minutes to midnight: 'This [election] is a crossroads in the history of our civilization that will determine whether or not we the people reclaim control over our government.' He then makes the link with Hillary Clinton and becomes even more explicit:

The Clinton machine is at the center of this power structure. We've seen this first hand in the Wikileaks documents, in which Hillary Clinton meets in secret with international banks to plot the destruction of US sovereignty in order to enrich these global financial powers, her special interest friends and her donors.

Here, Trump takes the final step towards a traditional conspiracy theory. Indeed, the second sentence of the quoted passage contains all the elements described in the first two chapters as characteristic of this pattern of thought. It claims that a group operating in secret (in this case Hillary Clinton and the international bankers, with all the implied Jewish associations), prompted by base motives (abolition of US sovereignty and self-enrichment) is pursuing a treacherous plan to control or destroy an institution, a country or indeed the entire world. Furthermore, it claims to offer evidence of its allegations (in this case the Wikileaks documents, i.e. the leaked internal memos of the conspirators). In the rest of his speech, Trump repeatedly presents himself as the victim of this conspiracy, vilified for standing up to the corrupt elites: 'Anyone who challenges their control is deemed a sexist, a racist, a xenophobe, and morally deformed.' At the same time, he promotes an image of himself as a classic renegade who has switched sides, a position he claims makes him uniquely suited to solving the crisis thanks to his familiarity with the corrupt elites: 'In my former life, I was an insider as much as anybody else. ... Now I'm being punished for leaving the special club and revealing to you the terrible things that are going on having to do with our country. Because I used to be part of the club, I'm the only one that can fix it.'[33]

This strategy clearly paid off. Trump won the election thanks to a small lead in key swing states such as Florida and Ohio, and above all in the Midwest, which has suffered particularly from the loss of traditional industries. As Jonathan T. Rothwell, head of the polling institute Gallup, shows in a major survey based on data gathered from 125,000 Americans, Trump's voters came from both above- and below-average income groups. What united them was a sense of lost status and social marginalization. Regardless of whether it affected them objectively, they felt that the country was changing steadily for the worse, and that they had been left behind culturally – the very conditions identified more generally in the previous chapter as a breeding ground for populism and conspiracism.[34]

That said, Trump's electoral success does not mean that conspiracy theories have been fully relegitimized. The main reason for his victory was the weakness of Hillary Clinton. To add two further caveats: firstly, as already mentioned, the majority of Trump's voters – even during the primaries – did not believe in conspiracy theories; it was rather that his populist rhetoric created a common platform both for these voters and those critical of the elites for other reasons. Secondly, Trump has been sharply criticized in the traditional media precisely because of his conspiracism. Numerous newspapers and magazines that normally abstain from endorsing a candidate voted not so much for Clinton as against Trump. The magazine *The Atlantic*, for example, which has only ever made two such endorsements in its long history, namely of Abraham Lincoln in 1860 and Lyndon B. Johnson in 1964, opted to throw its weight behind Clinton – a decision which, as in the case of other publications, was influenced in no small part by Trump's predilection for conspiracy theories.

This enduring stigmatization also explains why Trump toned down his conspiracist rhetoric again after the election. In an interview with the broadcaster ABC a few days afterwards, he once again raised the spectre of electoral fraud, but refrained from mentioning specifics when questioned further. Such a claim is more useful to him as a conspiracy rumour than as a fully formulated conspiracy theory. To date, therefore (June 2020), he has avoided being too explicit when it comes to conspiracy theories, even though Ukrainegate, which led to his impeachment, was motivated by a conspiracy theory that Trump obviously believes himself, namely that the then vice-president Joe Biden interfered in Ukrainian politics to protect his son Hunter. But despite making frequent allusions to this and other alleged plots and trotting out familiar memes, he no longer gets into elaborate theories.

Even in the USA, therefore, conspiracy theories have not yet regained the status they enjoyed for centuries throughout the Western world as a legitimate form of knowledge. To substantial sections of the public, they remain an absurdity that instantly undermines the credibility of the person uttering them. The trouble is, those particular sections of the public

– namely the traditional media and the academic community – have become less relevant and are rapidly losing their authority over the debate. As Katharina Thalmann pointedly puts it, 'conspiracy theory remains illegitimate [but] that might not matter anymore'.[35] Consequently – and this applies on both sides of the Atlantic – many important issues are no longer debated by society as a whole. Instead, subpublics have turned into echo chambers or even filter bubbles based on fundamentally contrasting assumptions, where arguments from outside can no longer penetrate or are no longer taken seriously. Needless to say, this is a serious problem for democratic societies.

Conclusion: When are conspiracy theories dangerous and what can we do about them?

On 30 April 2020, hundreds of protesters gathered outside the State Capitol in Lansing, Michigan, to demonstrate against the stay-at-home order issued by Democratic governor Gretchen Whitmer in an attempt to contain the spread of the coronavirus in the state. The protest was smaller than the one two weeks earlier, but the mood was far more aggressive. It was also at least in part fuelled by the widespread conspiracy theories that had been circulating about the coronavirus. The slogans many of the protesters chanted, the placards they carried, and their online communication in the days before the protest showed that a considerable number of them did not believe that the virus was real, or thought that it was no more dangerous than the common flu. Many thought that the hysteria over the virus was being purposely manufactured in order to hurt President Trump by way of damaging the economy, or to rob them of their constitutional rights.[1]

Accordingly, many of the protesters defied the rules of social distancing, and a considerable number of them carried firearms, among them many who managed to enter the Capitol building where the state assembly was debating the COVID-19 restrictions. Michigan is one of the US states that allows the open carrying of firearms, so the protesters were not in violation of the law. Yet the display of guns was clearly meant to send a message, and it achieved its desired effect. 'Directly above me, men with rifles yelling at us. Some of my colleagues who own bulletproof vests are wearing them. I have never appreciated our Sergeants-at-Arms more than today', tweeted one Senator. Governor Whitmer remained undeterred and extended the state of emergency. This angered President Trump, who was by this time already eager to end the lockdown throughout the United States to allow the economy to recover and thus to boost his re-election bid in the autumn. Unsurprisingly, he took to Twitter to call on the governor to 'give a little' and 'make a deal' with the protesters, whom he called 'very good people'. His language was far more restrained than it had been two weeks earlier – when he reacted to the first protests with the tweet 'LIBERATE MICHIGAN!', thus fuelling the far more aggressive atmosphere of 30 April – but it did little to defuse the tensions.[2]

To the best of my knowledge, nobody was hurt that day in Lansing, and at the time of writing we do not know if the protests led to a rise in COVID-19 infections. But the episode illustrates three out of the four major ways in which conspiracy theories can be dangerous: they can lead to radicalization and violence; they can make people disregard medical knowledge and, as a consequence, endanger themselves and others; and they can undermine trust in elected politicians and the democratic process as such. What the Lansing protests do not exemplify are crisis-actor conspiracy theories which claim that shootings and other kinds of attacks never really took place and were staged instead by sinister forces, usually the government or the 'deep state', using so-called crisis actors. Such conspiracy theories can cause severe distress to those who have lost loved ones in these tragic events.

The connection between conspiracy theories and violence has been on the public radar in many countries for quite some time. Indeed, in the USA, the authorities began to make serious efforts to deal with the militias – paramilitary organizations that feel threatened by the government and whose members often believe in the New World Order conspiracy – as far back as the mid-1990s. This movement became a focus of public attention following the attack on a government building in Oklahoma City on 19 April 1995, in which 168 people died. The ringleader, Timothy McVeigh, subscribed to numerous conspiracy theories; among his influences was the profoundly racist and anti-Semitic conspiracist novel *The Turner Diaries*. Such was the concern in the USA regarding the violent inclinations and misguided beliefs of these militias that a Senate Commission was set up to address the issue. Attacks such as that of autumn 2018 on the Tree of Life Synagogue in Pittsburgh, in which eleven people died, have continued to fuel the debate to this day.[3]

In Germany, the same debate began in October 2016, when a forty-nine-year-old man – a member of the sovereign citizen movement, which does not recognize the authority of the German government – shot at a team of police officers who had been sent to confiscate his weapons, killing one of them. It gained new traction three years later when a gunman, radicalized online through anti-Semitic conspiracy theories, tried to enter a synagogue in Halle during the Jewish holiday of Yom Kippur. When he couldn't break into the synagogue, he shot one passer-by on the pavement and a young man in a nearby kebab shop before being arrested.

In Britain, the June 2016 murder of Labour MP Jo Cox, whose killer regarded her as 'one of "the collaborators" [and] a traitor' to white people, made the public painfully aware of the harmful consequences of belief in conspiracy theories. In Norway, the discussion began after Anders Breivik murdered a total of seventy-seven people during attacks in Oslo and on the island of Utøya on 22 July 2011. Shortly before the shooting, Breivik had posted a 1,500-page manifesto on the internet setting out his version of the 'Great Replacement' conspiracy theory, as it has since been named. According to Breivik, radical Islamists were systematically infiltrating Europe in order to destroy Western culture, and European governments were party to this plot.[4]

The COVID-19 pandemic notwithstanding, the 'Great Replacement' theory is still the most prominent conspiracy theory currently circulating among white supremacists and right-wing populists all over the world. It claims that the white Christian populations of the Western world are being replaced by Muslim immigration. This immigration is often said to be orchestrated by a dubious financial elite (frequently, George Soros is blamed as the mastermind behind the plot) to achieve its sinister aims. The same conspiracy theory was so responsible for another recent devastating attack. On 15 March 2019, twenty-eight-year-old Australian Brenton Harrison Tarrant killed fifty-one people and injured almost as many at Al Noor Mosque and the Linwood Islamic Centre in Christchurch, New Zealand, when he opened fire on the Muslim congregations gathered there for Friday prayer. Before he left home for the attack, he emailed a seventy-eight-page manifesto entitled 'The Great Replacement' to New Zealand's prime minister and several media outlets, and shared links to the file via Twitter and 8chan.

Several studies have by now confirmed the link between conspiracy theories, radicalization and violence. In a study often cited in this context, Jamie Bartlett and Carl Miller of the British think-tank Demos assessed the conspiracist tendencies of fifty extremist groups around the world who have resorted to violent methods in the past. The authors argue that conspiracy theories are indeed a 'radicalizing multiplier': '[they] hold extremist groups together and push them in a more extreme and sometimes violent direction'. In much the same vein, Benjamin Lee has recently suggested that conspiracy theories are not only catalysts for radicalization but that they also have the function of 'preventing deradi-calisation' within extremist groups because they 'improve solidarity and insulate believers from external challenges to their ideas'.[5]

Most at risk of becoming the target of such conspiracist-induced violence are minorities and other already stigmatized groups, followed by representatives of the state and 'ordinary' politicians. As far as their personal safety is concerned, there is little danger for leaders such as Barack Obama or Angela Merkel. Conspiracy theorists may think that they are reptilians, members of the Illuminati, or complicit in the 'Great Replacement', but they are so well protected that assassination attempts on them are unlikely. Politicians like Jo Cox and the members of the Michigan legislature, however, are far more vulnerable, and the same goes for police officers and others who might be perceived as representatives of a thoroughly corrupt state. When the likes of Donald Trump add fuel to the fire via Twitter, the situation becomes particularly toxic.

Racism and anti-Semitism are of course also components

of anti-elitist conspiracy theories – see for example the Trump speech discussed in the previous chapter, in which he castigates (implicitly Jewish) bankers – but they are especially potent when directed at the weak and marginalized. In such contexts, conspiracy theories unquestionably have the capacity to reinforce existing prejudices and discrimination and so increase the potential for violence. As we saw in Chapter 3, they offer a rationalization for the accuser's own behaviour: if immigrants or representatives of other faiths are rejected or opposed, it is not because they are different, but because they are part of an insidious plan. The same is true in cases such as the European refugee crisis, where conspiracy theorists assume the existence of a collaboration between domestic elites and Muslim refugees. Although the former are the alleged puppet-masters, the latter are easier to target.

Conspiracy theories that deny established medical knowledge, such as those surrounding the coronavirus, occasionally have the potential to lead to violence, too, as the armed protests in Michigan show. But what is far more problematic about them is their ability to make those who believe in them endanger themselves and others involuntarily. This is not the case with conspiracy theories that falsely proclaim a virus to be particularly dangerous because it was allegedly manufactured in a biological weapons laboratory, as some people (still) believe about the HIV virus and now about the coronavirus. But it is a problem in the case of those who foster a false sense of security by claiming that diseases like COVID-19 or AIDS do not exist, and that the public is being deceived by sinister forces pursuing a hidden agenda. Vaccination conspiracy theories also fall into this category, whether they claim that vaccines can cause serious harm yet continue to be used for financial reasons, or maintain that vaccinations are used to implant chips allowing the conspirators to trace and control people.

People who believe that AIDS does not exist are more likely to contract the disease because they might not take the necessary precautions. By the same token, they are more likely to spread it once they have been diagnosed because they will not believe the diagnosis and may continue to have unprotected sexual intercourse. Similarly, people who believe that vaccinations are a tool used by evil conspirators to control or harm them and their families will refuse to have their children or themselves inoculated, thus endangering not only themselves and their offspring but also those who depend on herd immunity because they cannot get vaccinated for reasons of health and age. Those who do not believe that the coronavirus exists or think that COVID-19 is quite harmless also pose a danger to themselves and others because they are more likely to disregard distancing and hygiene rules. In fact, as the protests against lockdown measures in Europe and the USA prove, they may even consider violating these rules to be an act of civil disobedience.

Another danger of conspiracy theories is that they can lead to profound distrust in the political system and disrupt the democratic processes necessary to deal with the many challenges humanity faces in the twenty-first century. As Karen Douglas and Daniel Jolley found in a study on the social consequences of conspiracism, someone who believes that all or most politicians are the puppets of hidden evildoers who are using them to pursue their own sinister goals is highly likely to stop voting altogether at some point. Another finding of the study was that the belief that climate change is a lie designed to achieve some dark purpose can lead people to behave in a less environmentally friendly way. Such behaviour does not pose a direct risk to life and limb, but it has the potential to aggravate the crises we are currently witnessing in the democratic systems of Europe and North America. The same is true for the other option open to those who think that politics is just a sham. They may join populist movements or parties that present themselves as the only genuine alternative in a rotten political system or as the true voice of the people. As members of such movements, they may occasionally take their protests to the streets to exert pressure on those they perceive to be acting against the interests of the people. This is what happened in Michigan, where many of the armed protesters were firm supporters of Donald Trump. Behaviour of this kind is problematic because such populist movements are, as no one has demonstrated more forcefully than Jan-Werner Muller, always anti-pluralist and ultimately, therefore, often anti-democratic.[6]

Finally, so-called crisis-actor conspiracy theories can do a lot of harm to people who have lost loved ones in tragedies that, according to the conspiracy theorists, never really occurred but were staged for the media and public to further the goals of the conspirators. The term 'crisis actor' appears to have been coined in 2012 by James Tracy, then still a tenured professor of communications at Florida Atlantic University. Tracy, who later lost his job, claimed that the Sandy Hooks Elementary School massacre of 14 December 2012, when twenty-six people, among them twenty children, were killed, never took place. Tracy was joined by many other conspiracy theorists in making this allegation, among them Alex Jones, as discussed in Chapter 3. Since then, virtually all shootings in the USA and elsewhere have been followed by such claims. On 5 June 2020, German musician Xavier Naidoo even claimed in a Telegram Messenger post that George Floyd, the African American killed by a Minneapolis police officer who pressed his knee into Floyd's neck for more than eight minutes, was still alive and that the alleged killing was a false-flag operation.[7]

Such absurd claims could be dismissed with a shrug if many conspiracy theorists did not harass the families of those who have lost loved ones in the tragedies concerned. Conspiracy theorists like Tracy and Jones have accused the parents of the Sandy Hooks victims of faking their children's deaths, and at times even claimed that their children never existed. Others have attacked the families of the victims of other shootings. It is not hard to imagine the enormous suffering that this has caused parents, spouses and other relatives already working through the trauma of losing people dear to them.

Conspiracy theories, then, are dangerous, and belief in them can have grave consequences. As such, studies that highlight the evils of conspiracy theories have fallen on fertile ground in the media, particularly in recent years and never more so than in the COVID-19 crisis. Many journalists and other observers tend to pathologize and demonize them altogether. In some sections of the public, anti-conspiracism has reached panic proportions, sometimes leading to obsessive reporting on topics such as which politician believes in which conspiracy theory and how many theories of this kind Trump bandied about during the election campaign. Not that such scrutiny is without justification, of course – particularly in Germany, where the myth of the global Jewish conspiracy paved the way for the Holocaust. But is it really the case that all conspiracy theories are dangerous?

Once again – unsurprisingly – things are not so simple. As the preceding pages will have made clear, some conspiracy theories are extremely dangerous. Others, however, are not. There are plenty of people who believe in conspiracy theories and interact in virtual and real communities, but who show no inclination to violence, do not endanger others by doubting established medical knowledge, do not support right-wing populists, and do not harass the bereaved. The 9/11 Truth movement or believers in David Icke's reptilian theory are just two examples.

In fact, many of the academic studies that attest to the dangers of conspiracy theories are more complex than they are sometimes given credit for in the media. Bartlett and Miller, for example – whose study often tends to be read in an abridged and somewhat distorted form – emphasize the complexity of the relationship between conspiracy theories and violence. After all, just as there are conspiracist groups with no history of violence whatsoever, so there are plenty of examples of violent organizations in which conspiracy theories play no part, such as the IRA, for instance. In his survey of the link between conspiracism and radicalization, Benjamin Lee accordingly concludes that 'the exact role of conspiracy theory in radicalisation remains an open question'. And while there is a lot that we do not know about the shootings discussed above, it seems clear that in all cases it was not just belief in certain conspiracy theories that prompted the crime; there were other factors at play, too. Moreover, tragic though such incidents are for the victims and their families, they are, thankfully, extremely rare.[8]

Similarly, some of the psychological studies on the problematic consequences of conspiracism need to be taken with a pinch of salt. Extrapolating from the laboratory to the real world is no easy matter. Douglas and Jolley, for example, presented their undergraduates with texts containing either conspiracist or non-conspiracist ideas and interviewed them subsequently on their response. That young students will be inclined to believe what their professors give them to read, and to say as much when questioned by them, is only to be expected. Moreover, the interviews were conducted straight afterwards; how long the students maintained their beliefs and what actual consequences they produced was beyond the scope of the study.

It is therefore important not to panic when it comes to conspiracy theories. They need to be taken seriously, as their repercussions can clearly be problematic, but a degree of discrimination is also necessary. Whether conspiracy theories per se are dangerous is the wrong question. Quite apart from the fact that we need to specify what we mean by 'dangerous', it also depends on which conspiracy theories we are talking about, whom they are directed at, who believes them and who voices them, since – as we saw in Chapter 3 – these are not necessarily the same people. Equally important are contextual factors: are conspiracy theories regarded as legitimate or illegitimate knowledge in the given context? How popular are they? Are they spread via official or alternative channels? Do they draw on existing prejudices against minorities or elites? If so, do they put a new spin on them? And what effects do they have in the case in question? In short, it will always depend on the concrete situation.

Nevertheless, given that some types of conspiracy theory can have alarming consequences, and that all conspiracy theories stand in the way of a proper understanding of reality, the question is what do to about them.

The discouraging cliché that hardened conspiracy theorists cannot be reached with arguments is, alas, all too true. This resistance to any attempt at falsification is due to the fact that – as discussed in Chapter 1 – conspiracy theorists generally work on an entirely different set of basic assumptions from those who don't believe in large-scale plots. Consequently, although a dialogue is possible in theory, it will not normally yield the desired results. In fact, empirical studies have shown that confronting conspiracy theorists with conclusive counterarguments only confirms them in their beliefs. This is because conspiracy theories – as we saw in Chapter 3 – fulfil a hugely important function in terms of their followers' identity. To challenge the theory is to shatter the self-image of the person you are attempting to persuade. That may be gratifying for the challenger, but it serves little purpose beyond that of self-affirmation.[9]

Any education campaign should therefore be aimed at those

who have already encountered the explanations offered by conspiracy theories but are not yet convinced. Provided certain ground rules are observed, this approach has a reasonable chance of success.[10] It is important, for example, not to dwell too much on the assumptions you are attempting to refute, lest these – rather than the non-conspiracist explanation – become fixed in your interlocutor's mind. Naturally, it is impossible to argue the case without making explicit reference to the conspiracy theory and its supposedly clinching arguments. But this should only be done briefly, after presenting the better explanation and making it clear that you are merely summarizing false information. Another reason for concentrating on the counter-narrative is that it offers the other party a way of making sense of events, this being – as noted in Chapter 3 – one of the main attractions of conspiracy theories. Lastly, it is important to restrict yourself to the key arguments, as too many details can produce the opposite effect.

Moreover, research has shown that it makes a lot of sense to 'inoculate' people against specific conspiracy theories. This 'prebunking', as it is also called, usually consists of two steps. First, the target audience needs to be alerted to the dangers of a specific conspiracy theory; second, and crucially, the logical flaws and contradictions in its arguments need to be exposed. As Jolley and Douglas have demonstrated, such an approach does indeed ensure that people are no longer negatively affected when they later come into contact with the actual conspiracy theory.[11]

However, such attempts at debunking and prebunking are inevitably reactive and/or limited to a specific conspiracy theory. It therefore seems much more worthwhile to equip people with the ability to distinguish between conspiracist and non-conspiracist explanations themselves. As already stated in Chapter 3, I am convinced that the discrepancies between different empirical studies on the correlation between education and conspiracism (some see an inverse relationship here, while others do not) can be explained by the fact that these surveys only consider people's *level* of education without examining *what* they have actually learned. I would argue that people familiar with the insights of modern social sciences, cultural studies or psychology are less inclined towards conspiracism than those who are comparatively ignorant of these disciplines and hence still adhere, implicitly or explicitly, to an old-fashioned understanding of human agency and social processes. A highly desirable goal, therefore, would be to teach more people the necessary social literacy at school and university.

This social literacy would form the cornerstone of a strategy designed to curb the spread of conspiracy theories, but would need to be complemented by two other essential elements which I would describe as media literacy and historical literacy. In the current situation, where the watchdog role of the media and the interpretative authority of traditional elites such as the academic community have sharply declined, and the seductive explanations offered by conspiracy theories are accessible at will via real and virtual alternative channels, the importance of media literacy should be only too clear. We have all had to learn – and must go on learning – to discriminate between reliable and unreliable sources of information, and to recognize the difference between someone's personal YouTube channel or blog and the website of a quality newspaper. We need to realize that the results of our Google searches and Facebook newsfeeds do not reflect reality but, to a large extent, our personal preferences, and that news that spreads fast may be popular but is not necessarily true. In other words, we need to learn and, above all, teach young people how the internet works and how it generates meaning.

The kind of media literacy I envisage is thus very general, and not specially geared to conspiracy theories. As for my notion of historical literacy, it too should have a general component, but alongside more specific aspects. Often, conspiracy theorists themselves point to historical experience in order to prove that conspiracies have existed and that many theories about them – Watergate being probably the most popular example – have turned out in retrospect to be true. The first point is correct; the second is not. There have always been conspiracy theories and always will be but, as we saw in Chapter 1, historically documented cases differ significantly in terms of scope, impact and effectiveness from the assumptions of conspiracy theorists about how plots work and what they can achieve. It would be important to communicate this by way of examples – and this is where historical literacy would overlap with social literacy. Convinced conspiracy theorists will probably groan at the manifesto I am outlining here, and I would therefore like to make it absolutely clear that I am not talking about an uncritical acceptance of established interpretations and submission to traditional authorities, but the empowerment of people to think for themselves and reach their own judgements, based on rational assumptions about human nature and social processes. These are precisely what conspiracy theories lack – yet they are a vital tool if we are to carry conviction when exercising the urgently necessary critique of power structures and those wielding power. A further problem of conspiracy theories – particularly those directed at elites – is that their often legitimate concerns and justified complaints are easily dismissed because of the problematic paradigm through which they are articulated. In terms of the 9/11 attacks, for example, there is a great deal to criticize in the conduct of the Bush administration, from the restriction of civil rights in the USA to the invasion of Iraq. But to formulate such criticism as a conspiracy theory according to which the government not only instrumentalized but actually carried out the attacks is to undermine even the justifiable elements of one's own critique.

But what is the best way to approach die-hard conspiracy theorists who – at least initially – are not open to conclusive arguments? Once again, there is no sure-fire solution: it all depends on the situation. Key factors are the nature of the conspiracy theory itself, its impact on the life of the conspiracy theorist and those around them, and their relationship to the challenger. There are good reasons not to talk to people who spread racist, sexist or anti-Semitic conspiracy theories, in the interests of avoiding an erosion of the boundaries of acceptable speech. Even so, it is important not to project such characteristics onto their theories. Not everyone who believes that the world is controlled by international bankers is a confirmed anti-Semite. Many modern conspiracy theories admit such interpretations, but do not insist on them. As such, wading in with accusations of anti-Semitism or racism is unlikely to be conducive to success.

Applying stigmatized labels such as 'paranoid' or 'conspiracy theorist' to the other party will have a similar effect. Rather than attacking the fundamental assumptions of their ideology from the outset, it probably makes more sense to begin with a more low-key approach, such as enquiring after the sources of some of their statements or detailed allegations. From my own experience, I can say that there is often a lot to be gained by simply listening in the first instance, since many conspiracy theorists feel – not always unreasonably – that they are not taken seriously outside their own echo chambers. My approach nowadays is to respond at least briefly to the critical emails I generally receive after lectures and interviews unless they are downright abusive. There is nearly always a degree of imbalance in this communication in that I may write ten lines after three days or so, only to receive a ten-page reply in the space of three hours, and I doubt that I have ever succeeded in bringing anyone round to my point of view in such an exchange. But the fact that I bothered to reply at all has often prompted such a positive reaction that this can be a first step in itself – and perhaps a tiny contribution towards solving what I regard as the most urgent problem in this context.

In Chapter 2, I dealt in some detail with Abraham Lincoln's famous 'House Divided' speech. Lincoln was firmly convinced that a society where slavery is legal in some regions and illegal in others could not survive in the long term. What advocates of slavery and their opponents shared, however, was a view of the world in which major conspiracies were par for the course. They disagreed over exactly who was pulling the strings, but were united in believing that this was how the world worked. That consensus no longer exists, and – in Western societies at least – we too are increasingly living in 'divided houses'. Publics in which conspiracy theories are still stigmatized coexist with publics where they have undergone a relegitimization. This fragmentation of society, as described in Chapter 5, does not necessarily follow ideological lines, but rather stems from radically differing assumptions about how history and society operate. It is this fragmentation that seems to me to be the real problem we are facing today, and it is particularly apparent in the context of conspiracy theories. As such, the current debate, that sees some sectors of the public panicking over conspiracies and others over conspiracy theories, is symptomatic of a deeper crisis afflicting democratic societies. After all, if societies can no longer agree on what is true, they will not be able to resolve the pressing problems of the twenty-first century.

Notes

Introduction

1 Churchill, W., 'Zionism versus Bolshevism: a Struggle for the Soul of the Jewish People', *Illustrated Sunday Herald*, 8 February 1920, p. 5, at https://en.wikisource.org/wiki/Zionism_versus_Bolshevism.

2 Lee, M. F., *Conspiracy Rising: Conspiracy Thinking and American Public Life*, Santa Barbara, CA: Praeger, 2011, pp. 62–3.

3 Grey Ellis, E., 'Coronavirus Conspiracy Theories are a Public Health Hazard', *Wired*, 27 March 2020, at https://www.wired.com/story/coronavirus-covid-19-misinformation-campaigns.

4 Hofstadter, R., 'The Paranoid Style in American Politics', in *The Paranoid Style in American Politics and Other Essays*, Cambridge, MA: Harvard University Press, 1996 [1964], pp. 3–40.

5 Edsall, T. B., 'The Paranoid Style in American Politics is Back', *New York Times*, 8 September 2016, at https://www.nytimes.com/2016/09/08/opinion/campaign-stops/the-paranoid-style-in-american-politics-is-back.html; Musgrave, P., 'Donald Trump is Normalizing Paranoia and Conspiracy Thinking in U.S. Politics', *Washington Post*, 12 January 2017, at https://www.washingtonpost.com/posteverything/wp/2017/01/12/donald-trump-has-brought-us-the-american-style-in-paranoid-politics/?utm_term=.dee6f1f76c8f; Lynch, C., 'Paranoid Politics: Donald Trump's Style Perfectly Embodies the Theories of Renowned Historian', *Salon*, 7 July 2017, at http://www.salon.com/2016/07/07/paranoid_politics_donald_trumps_style_perfectly_embodies_the_theories_of_renowned_historian; Heer, J., 'Donald Trump's United States of Conspiracy', *New Republic*,

14 June 2016, at https://newrepublic.com/article/134257/ donald-trumps-united-states-conspiracy; Clinton, H., 'His Disregard for the Values that Make Our Country Great Is Profoundly Dangerous', 25 August 2016, campaign speech in Reno, NV, at https://www.hillaryclinton.com/post/ remarks-on-trumps-prejudice-and-paranoia-in-reno-nv.

6 Jacobsen, L., 'Das Trump-Puzzle: Angstpolitik', *Zeit online*, 3 November 2016, at http://www.zeit.de/politik/ ausland/2016-10/donald-trump-puzzle-phaenomen-us-wahl-populismus; Lepenies, W., 'Die Politik der Paranoia erreicht jetzt auch uns', *Welt.de*, 10 March 2016, at https://www. welt.de/debatte/kommentare/article153103845/Die-Politik-der-Paranoia-erreicht-jetzt-auch-uns.html; Stein, H., 'Der gefährliche Glaube an die große Verschwörung', *Welt.de*, 11 September 2016, at https://www.welt.de/debatte/kommentare/ article157942289/Der-gefaehrliche-Glaube-an-die-grosse-Verschwoerung.html; Hyde, M., 'A Waco Week, as Corbynistas Do Politics in The Paranoid Style', *Guardian*, 3 August 2018, at https://www.theguardian.com/commentisfree/2018/aug/03/ corbynistas-politics-labour-leader.

7 For the USA, see Oliver, E. and Wood, T., 'Conspiracy Theories and the Paranoid Style(s) of Mass Opinion', *American Journal of Political Science* 58(4), 2014: pp. 952–66; for Europe, see Drochon, H., 'Who Believes in Conspiracy Theories in Great Britain and Europe?', in Uscinski, J. (ed.) *Conspiracy Theories and the People Who Believe Them*, New York: Oxford University Press, 2019, pp. 337–46.

Chapter 1

1 Barkun, M., *A Culture of Conspiracy: Apocalyptic Visions in Contemporary America*, 2nd edn., Berkeley: University of California Press, 2013, pp. 1–14; Cubitt, G., 'Conspiracy Myths and Conspiracy Theories', *Journal of Anthropological Society of Oxford* 20(1), 1989: pp. 12–26.

2 See Oberhauser, C., 'Nesta Helen Webster (1876–1960)', in Reinalter, H. (ed.) *Handbuch der Verschwörungstheorien*, Leipzig: Salier, 2018, pp. 319–26.

3 Webster, N. H., *The French Revolution: A Study in Democracy*, London: Constable, 1919; *The French Terror and Russian Bolshevism*, London: Boswell, 1920; *World Revolution: The Plot Against Civilization*, London: Small, Maynard & Company, 1921; *Secret Societies and Subversive Movements*, London: Boswell, 1924. For an analysis of her conspiracy theories and

their impact, see Lee, M. F., *Conspiracy Rising: Conspiracy Thinking and American Public Life*, Santa Barbara, CA: Praeger, 2011.

4 See Olmsted, K. S., *Real Enemies: Conspiracy Theories and American Democracy, World War I to 9/11*, Oxford: Oxford University Press, 2009, p. 4.

5 Von Bieberstein, J. R., *Die These von der Verschwörung, 1776–1945: Philosophen, Freimaurer, Juden, Liberale und Sozialisten als Verschwörer gegen die Sozialordnung*, Bern: Lang, 1976.

6 Lincoln, A., Campaign Speech, 16 June 1858, Springfield, IL, at http://teachingamericanhistory.org/library/document/house-divided-speech.

7 Barkun, *A Culture of Conspiracy*, p. 6.

8 Pfahl-Traughber, A., '"Bausteine" zu einer Theorie über "Verschwörungstheorien": Definition, Erscheinungsformen, Funktionen und Ursachen', in Reinhalter, H. (ed.) *Verschwörungstheorien: Theorie – Geschichte – Wirkung*, Innsbruck: StudienVerlag, 2002, p. 31.

9 Pfahl-Traughber, '"Bausteine" zu einer Theorie über "Verschwörungstheorien"', p. 31.

10 Keeley, B. L., 'Of Conspiracy Theories', in Coady, D. (ed.) *Conspiracy Theories: The Philosophical Debate*, rev. edn., Aldershot: Ashgate, 2006 [1999], p. 58.

11 Grimes, D. R., 'On the Viability of Conspiratorial Beliefs', *PLOS ONE* 11(3), 2016, doi: 10.1371/journal.pone.0147905.

12 Keeley, 'Of Conspiracy Theories', p. 58.

13 Byford, J., *Conspiracy Theories: A Critical Introduction*, Basingstoke: Palgrave Macmillan, 2011, p. 33.

14 Popper, K., *The High Tide of Prophecy: Hegel, Marx, and the Aftermath*, 4th and rev. edn., Vol. 2 of *The Open Society and Its Enemies*, London: Routledge, 1962 [1945], p. 93 (italics in original).

15 Popper, *The High Tide of Prophecy*, pp. 94, 95 (italics in original).

16 For an overview of the conspiracy theories on the assassination, see Knight, P., *The Kennedy Assassination*, Edinburgh: Edinburgh University Press, 2007, pp. 75–104.

17 Many of these superconspiracy theories were first published in Steve Weissman's anthology *Big Brother and the Holding Company: The World behind Watergate*, Palo Alto: Ramparts Press, 1974. Jim Hougan presents Nixon as a victim of the Secret Service who staged the affair to keep a CIA-operated call girl ring secret. See Hougan, *Secret Agenda: Watergate, Deep Throat,*

and the CIA, New York: Random House, 1984. For a discussion of how the Senate Committee and the journalist tried to avoid being perceived as conspiracy theorists, see Thalmann, K., *The Stigmatization of Conspiracy Theory since the 1950s: 'A Plot to Make Us Look Foolish'*, London: Routledge, 2019, pp. 153–8.

18 Cassam, Q., *Conspiracy Theories*, Cambridge: Polity Press, 2019, p. 7.

19 McKenzie-McHarg, A., 'Conspiracy Theory: the Nineteenth-Century Prehistory of a Twentieth-Century Concept', in Uscinski, J. (ed.) *Conspiracy Theories and the People Who Believe Them*. Oxford: Oxford University Press, 2019, pp. 62–81.

20 Knight, P., *Conspiracy Culture: From Kennedy to* The X Files, London: Routledge, 2000, p. 11.

21 Fenster, M., *Conspiracy Theories: Secrecy and Power in American Culture*, 2nd edn., Minneapolis: University of Minnesota Press, 2008, p. 242; Herman, E., 'Einwanderungs-Chaos: Was ist der Plan?', *Wissensmanufaktur*, 22 August 2015, at http://www.wissensmanufaktur.net/einwanderungs-chaos.

22 '187 radical organizations', in the comments to C. Spiering, 'John Podesta Fuels Russian Conspiracy Theory: Urges Electoral College to Revisit Election', *Breitbart*, 12 December 2016, https://www.breitbart.com/politics/2016/12/12/john-podesta-fuels-russian-conspiracy-theory-urges-electoral-college-revisit-election/

23 See, for example, this article, which also repro-duces images of the memo: 'CIA Memo 1967: CIA Coined & Weaponized the Label "Conspiracy Theory"', at https://steemit.com/history/@thelastheretik/cia-coined-and-weaponized-the-label-conspiracy-theory.

24 See, for example, Räikkä, J. and Basham, L., 'Conspiracy Theory Phobia', in Uscinski, J. (ed.) *Conspiracy Theories and the People Who Believe Them*, New York: Oxford University Press, 2019, pp. 178–86.

25 Bratich, J. Z., *Conspiracy Panics: Political Rationality and Popular Culture*, Albany: SUNY Press, 2008, p. 4.

26 An entire Wikipedia article is dedicated to this alleged connection: https://en.wikipedia.org/wiki/Saddam_Hussein_and_al-Qaeda_link_allegations.

27 For the classic definition of conspiracy theories as counter-narratives, see Fiske, J., *Media Matters: Everyday Culture and Political Change*, Minneapolis: University of Minnesota Press, 1994. For studies that demonstrate that outside of the West conspiracy theories are often the official version of events, see, for example, Borenstein, E., *Plots against Russia: Conspiracy*

and Fantasy after Socialism, Ithaca, NY: Cornell University Press, 2019; and Gray, M., *Conspiracy Theories in the Arab World: Sources and Politics*, London: Routledge, 2010.

28 Boyer, P. S. and Nissenbaum, S., *Salem Possessed: The Social Origins of Witchcraft*, Cambridge, MA: Harvard University Press, 1974.
29 Pfahl-Traughber, '"Bausteine" zu einer Theorie über "Verschwörungstheorien"', p. 31.
30 Hepfer, K., *Verschwörungstheorien: Eine philosophische Kritik der Unvernunft*, Bielefeld: Transcript, 2015, p. 24.

Chapter 2

1 Fenster, M., *Conspiracy Theories: Secrecy and Power in American Culture*, 2nd edn., Minneapolis: University of Minnesota Press, 2008, p. 119.
2 Avery, D., *Loose Change Final Cut* (2007), at https://www.youtube.com/watch?v=YmYgGAlG0sY. The original version of Loose Change is no longer available on YouTube. The later versions are easy to find with the search function.
3 Fenster, *Conspiracy Theories*, p. 94 (italics in original).
4 Hepfer, K., *Verschwörungstheorien: Eine philosophische Kritik der Unvernunft*, Bielefeld: Transcript, 2015, p. 37; Caruana, S., 'A Skeleton Key to the Gemstone File', in *The Gemstone File: A Memoir*, Victoria: Trafford Press, 2006, pp. 61–97.
5 Hofstadter, R., 'The Paranoid Style in American Politics', in *The Paranoid Style in American Politics and Other Essays*, Cambridge, MA: Harvard University Press, 1996 [1964], pp. 3–40, p. 37.
6 Byford, J., *Conspiracy Theories: A Critical Introduction*, Basingstoke: Palgrave Macmillan, 2011, p. 89.
7 McKenzie-McHarg, A., 'Experts Versus Eyewitnesses: Or, How Did Conspiracy Theories Come to Rely on Images?', *Word & Image* 35(2), 2019: pp. 141–58.
8 Agent S, 'Body Double – PROOF!', *YouTube*, 14 September 2016, at https://www.youtube.com/watch?v=1w3NFTzyMmg&t.
9 Hofstadter, 'The Paranoid Style in American Politics', p. 85.
10 Budenz, L., *Men without Faces: The Communist Conspiracy in the United States*, New York: Harper, 1950; Monk, M., *Awful Disclosures of the Hotel Dieu Nunnery of Montreal*, 2nd edn., London: Hodson, 1837 [1836].
11 Cf. Wisnewski, G., *2017 – Das andere Jahrbuch: verheimlicht – vertuscht – vergessen: was 2016 nicht in der Zeitung stand*, Rottenburg am Neckar: Kopp, 2016; or, Wisnewski,

G., *Drahtzieher der Macht: die Bilderberger – Verschwörung der Spitzen von Wirtschaft, Politik, und Medien*, Munich: Knaur, 2010; Bröckers, M., *Der Fall Ken Jebsen oder Wie Journalismus im Netz seine Unabhängigkeit zurückgewinnen kann*, Frankfurt am Main: fifty-fifty, 2016; or, Bröckers, M. and Walther, C. C., *11.9. – Zehn Jahre Danach: Der Einsturz eines Lügengebäudes*, Frankfurt am Main: Westend, 2011; Ganser, D., 'Die Terroranschläge vom 11. September 2001 und der "Clash of Civilizations" – Warum die Friedensforschung medial vermittelte Feindbilder hinterfragen muss', *YouTube*, 15 December 2014, at https://www.youtube.com/watch?v=cgkQXJ3mugY; Factbase Videos, 'InfoWars: Alex Jones Interviews Donald Trump – December 2, 2015', *YouTube*, 3 November 2017, at https://www.youtube.com/watch?v=4LeChPL0sLE; ABC News, 'Donald Trump Full Speech at Florida Rally', *YouTube*, 13 October 2016, at https://www.youtube.com/watch?v=Wuy1M05DM38.

12 Horn, E. and Hagemeister, M., 'Ein Stoff für Bestseller', in Horn and Hagemeister, *Die Fiktion von der jüdischen Weltverschwörung: zu Text und Kontext der 'Protokolle der Weisen von Zion'* [The Fiction of the Jewish World Conspiracy: On the Text and Context of the 'Protocols of the Elders of Zion'], Göttingen: Wallstein, 2012, pp. x–xi; vii–xxii.

13 Lincoln, A., Campaign Speech, 16 June 1858, Springfield, IL, at http://teachingamericanhistory.org/library/document/house-divided-speech (italics in original).

14 The 'umbrella man' was identified as Louis Steven Witt. He claimed to have wanted to remind JFK that his father, Joseph Kennedy, showed initial sympathy with the Nazis and had admired the British Prime Minister Neville Chamberlain, whose hallmark had been a black umbrella. *The New York Times* produced a short documentary about Witt in 2011, entitled *The Umbrella Man*.

15 Keeley, B., 'Of Conspiracy Theories', in Coady, D. (ed.) *Conspiracy Theories: The Philosophical Debate*, Aldershot: Ashgate, 2006, pp. 45–60. See pp. 52–5 for a comprehensive discussion of this topic. For a discussion of the Kennedy example, see Coady, D., 'Conspiracy Theories and Official Stories', in the same volume, pp. 115–27, in particular, pp. 119–20. For a different take on the issue, see Dentith, M., *The Philosophy of Conspiracy Theories*, Basingstoke: Palgrave Macmillan, 2014, pp. 124–43.

16 ABC News, 'Hillary Clinton Pneumonia Diagnosis Revealed', *YouTube*, 11 September 2016, at https://www.youtube.com/watch?v=LCTqIlXOVF0; The Alex Jones Channel,

'Perhaps They Reported Something That Wasn't Supposed to Be Reported Yet: ABC Nightly News Reports Hillary's Death', *YouTube*, 12 September 2016, at https://www.youtube.com/watch?v=oNBRZX-f9MQ; Gerhard Wisnewski, 'Was ist dran: US-TV erklärt Hillary Clinton für tot', *YouTube*, 17 September 2016, at https://www.youtube.com/watch?v=3uYvCMrjXU8&t=419s.

17 Bröckers and Walther, *11.9. – zehn Jahre danach*, p. 19.

18 Byford, *Conspiracy Theories*, p. 91.

19 Ganser postulates the central control of such paramilitary units in Europe by NATO and, ultimately, the CIA, although there is no evidence for this. He also interprets his sources very one-sidedly, makes no serious attempt at source analysis, and in one case relies on a source – a particular version of the US army manual – that was exposed as a KGB forgery long before he began his research into the subject; cf. Davies, P., 'Review of Ganser, *NATO's Secret Armies*', *Journal of Strategic Studies* 28(6), 2006: pp. 1064–68; Hansen, P. H., 'Daniele Ganser: *NATO's Secret Armies: Operation Gladio and Terrorism in Western Europe*', *Journal of Intelligence History* 5(1), 2007: p. 111; see also Hansen, 'Falling Flat on the Stay-behinds', *International Journal of Intelligence and Counter Intelligence* 19(1), 2006: pp. 182–6; Riste, O., 'Review of Ganser, *NATO's Secret Armies*', *Intelligence and National Security* 20(3), 2005: pp. 550–1; Riste, '"Stay Behind": A Clandestine Cold War Phenomenon', *Journal of Cold War Studies* 16(4), 2014: pp. 35–59; Cogan, C. G., '"Stay-Behind" in France: Much Ado About Nothing?', *Journal of Strategic Studies* 30(6), 2007: pp. 937–54.

20 All questions about the collapse of WTC 7 are comprehensively answered in a special FAQ section on NIST's website: https://www.nist.gov/topics/disaster-failure-studies/faqs-nist-wtc-7-investigation.

21 Since this book went into production, Ganser has revised his stance on 9/11 ever so slightly. After the publication of the Hulsey Report in September 2019 – a research project funded by the 9/11 Truth Movement – Ganser began to claim that it had now been proven without any doubt that WTC 7 was brought down by controlled demolition. He continues, however, to pretend that he is just asking questions because he still does not claim explicitly that the Bush administration did it. He simply insinuates this just as strongly as before.

22 Mather, C., *Wonders of the Invisible World*, Boston: no publisher, 1693, p. 14; Barruel quoted in Byford, *Conspiracy Theories*, p.

75; Morse, S. F. B., *Foreign Conspiracy against the Liberties of the United States*, 7th edn., New York: American and Foreign Christian Union, 1855 [1835], pp. 93, 99; a collection of similar statements by Jones can be found in the video 'Trump Ally Alex Jones: Clinton, Obama Are Demons', *mediamatters4america*, 10 October 2016, at https://www.youtube.com/watch?v=M5KTiAcTEyc.

23　Herman, E., 'Flüchtlingschaos', *Wissensmanufaktur*, 22 August 2015, at http://www.wissensmanufaktur.net/einwanderungs-chaos; on Obama and the New World Order, see e.g. 'Globalist Puppet Obama EXPOSED', *UrbanWarfareChannel*, 12 June 2011, at https://www.youtube.com/watch?v=Lc5io4LOfTQ.

24　Mather, *Wonders of the Invisible World*, p. 45; Beecher, L., *A Plea for the West*, New York: Truman & Smith, 1835, p. 56; Morse, *Foreign Conspiracy against the Liberties of the United States*, p. 100; Herman, 'Flüchtlingschaos'.

25　Mather, *Wonders of the Invisible World*, pp. 37, 56, 83, 97; Dondero, G. A., 'Communism in Our Schools', in *Appendix to Records of the 2nd Session of the 79th US Congress*, vol. 92(11), Washington: GPO, 1946, p. 3516; Hoover, J. E., *Masters of Deceit: the Story of Communism in America and How to Fight It*, New York: Holt, 1958, pp. 81, 188; Budenz, L., *The Techniques of Communism*, Chicago: Regnery, 1954, p. 318; Starck, J. A., *Der Triumph der Philosophie im Achtzehnten Jahrhunderte 1*, Germantown (Augsburg), 1803, p. 208; Barruel, A., *Memoirs Illustrating the History of Jacobinism 1*, London: Hudson & Goodwin, 1799 [1797], p. xvi.

26　Morse, *Foreign Conspiracy against the Liberties of the United States*, p. 44; 'InfoWars: Alex Jones Interviews Donald Trump – December 2, 2015', *Factbase Videos*, 3 November 2017, at https://www.youtube.com/watch?v=4LeChPL0sLE.

27　Morse, *Foreign Conspiracy against the Liberties of the United States*, p. 100; Beecher, *A Plea for the West*, p. 114; Herman, 'Flüchtlingschaos'.

28　At https://i.pinimg.com/736x/0f/0b/9c/0f0b9cf9b65ac82a1cb 2a4816c9c8a7c--conspiracy-theories-pay-attention-anarchist-quotes.jpg; on Danny Casolaro, see https://en.wikipedia.org/wiki/Danny_Casolaro.

29　'Alex Jones Goes Nuts on the BBC and Host Calls Him an Idiot & "Worst Person Ever Interviewed"', YouTube, 9 June 2013, at https://www.youtube.com/watch?v=Ch9gQ9JOe3Y.

30　Hofstadter, 'The Paranoid Style in American Politics', p. 31.

31　Ernst, M. L. and Loth, D., *Report on the American Communist*, New York: Holt, 1952, p. 127; on this, see also Butter, M.,

Plots, Designs, and Schemes: American Conspiracy Theories from the Puritans to the Present, Berlin: de Gruyter, 2014, pp. 243–8.
32 Hofstadter, 'The Paranoid Style in American Politics', p. 21.

Chapter 3

1 For studies that continue to associate belief in conspiracy theories with mental illness, see Ramsay, R., *Conspiracy Theories*, Harpenden: Pocket Essentials, 2006; and Barron, D., Morgan, K. D., Towell, A., Altemeyer, B. and Swami, V., 'Associations between Schizotypy and Belief in Conspiracist Ideation', *Personality and Individual Differences* 70, 2014: pp. 156–9. For studies that show how widespread conspiracy theories actually are, see, for example, Oliver, E. and Wood, T., 'Conspiracy Theories and the Paranoid Style(s) of Mass Opinion', *American Journal of Political Science* 58(4), 2014: pp. 952–66; and Zick, A., Beate, K. and Berghan, W., *Verlorene Mitte – Feindselige Zustände: Rechtsextreme Einstellungen in Deutschland 2018/19*, Bonn: Dietz, 2019.
2 McCarthy, J., *McCarthyism: The Fight for America – Documented Answers to Questions Asked by Friend and Foe*, New York: Devin-Adair, 1952, p. 18.
3 The psychological research on conspiracy theories is concisely summarized in Douglas K., Sutton, R. M., Chichocka, A., Nefes T., Chee Siang Ang and Deravi, F., 'Understanding Conspiracy Theories', *Advances in Political Psychology* 40, 2019, doi: 10.1111/pops.12568. Brotherton, R., *Suspicious Minds: Why We Believe Conspiracy Theories*, New York: Bloomsbury, 2015, provides another excellent overview; see pp. 159–79 for a discussion of pattern recognition and pp. 181–201 for the human need to ascribe intentionality; Van Prooijen, J.-W., *The Psychology of Conspiracy Theories*, London: Routledge, 2018 is another very good introduction to the psychological underpinnings of conspiracism. See pp. 40–8 for pattern perception and intentionalism.
4 Brotherton, *Suspicious Minds*, p. 171.
5 See Van Prooijen, *The Psychology of Conspiracy Theories*, pp. 25–32.
6 Melley, T., 'Brainwashed! Conspiracy Theory and Ideology in the Postwar United States', *New German Critique* 35(1), 2008: pp. 145–64.
7 Girard, R., *The Scapegoat*, Baltimore: Johns Hopkins University Press, 1986.

8 Rozsa, M., 'Qanon Is the Conspiracy Theory that Won't Die: Here's What They Believe, and Why They're Wrong', *Salon*, 18 August 2019, at https://www.salon.com/2019/08/18/qanon-is-the-conspiracy-theory-that-wont-die-heres-what-they-believe-and-why-theyre-wrong.

9 Groh, D., 'Die verschwörungstheoretische Versuchung', in *Anthropologische Dimensionen der Geschichte*, Frankfurt am Main: Suhrkamp, 1992, p. 274.

10 Hofstadter, R., 'The Paranoid Style in American Politics', in *The Paranoid Style in American Politics and Other Essays*, Cambridge, MA: Harvard University Press, 1996 [1964], p. 30.

11 For the most comprehensive overview of quantitative research on the subject, see Brotherton, *Suspicious Minds*. For studies that find that conspiracy theories appeal more to men, see Marchlewska, M., Chichocka, A., Łozowsk, F., Górska, P. and Winiewski, M., 'In Search of an Imaginary Enemy: Catholic Collective Narcissism and the Endorsement of Gender Conspiracy Beliefs', *The Journal of Social Psychology* 159, 2019: pp. 1–14; and Zick, A., Küpper, B. and Berghan, W., *Verlorene Mitte – Feindselige Zustände: rechtsextreme Einstellungen in Deutschland 2018/19*, Bonn: Dietz, 2019. For studies that come to the opposite conclusion, see Bartoschek, S., *Bekanntheit von und Zustimmung zu Verschwörungstheorien: eine Empirische Grundlagenarbeit*, Hanover: JMB Verlag, 2015 [2013]; as well as Bruder, M., Haffke, P., Neave, N., Nouripanah, N. and Imhoff, R., 'Measuring Individual Differences in Generic Beliefs in Conspiracy Theories Across Cultures: Conspiracy Mentality Questionnaire', *Frontiers in Psychology* 4(225), 2013. For the argument that a higher level of education decreases the tendency to conspiracism, see Uscinski, J. E. and Parent, J. M., *American Conspiracy Theories*, Oxford: Oxford University Press, 2014, p. 86; Douglas, K., Sutton, R. M., Callan, M. J., Dawtry, R. J. and Harvey, A. J., 'Someone is Pulling the Strings: Hypersensitive Agency Detection and Belief in Conspiracy Theories', *Thinking and Reasoning* 22, 2016: pp. 57–77; and Van Prooijen, J.-W., 'Why Education Predicts Decreased Belief in Conspiracy Theories', *Applied Cognitive Psychology* 31(1), 2016: pp. 50–8; for the result that there is no connection, see the seminal study by Goertzel, T., 'Belief in Conspiracy Theories', *Political Psychology* 15, 1994: pp. 733–44; as well as Imhoff, R. and Bruder, M., 'Speaking (Un-)truth to Power: Conspiracy Mentality as a Generalized Political Attitude', *European Journal of Personality* 28(1), 2013: pp. 25–43.

12 Goertzel, 'Belief in Conspiracy Theories'; the aspect of

powerlessness is covered in, among others, the influential study by Abalakina-Paap, M., Stephan, W. G., Craig, T. and Gregory, W. L., 'Beliefs in Conspiracies', *Political Psychology* 20(3), 1999: pp. 637–47.

13 Uscinski and Parent, *American Conspiracy Theories*, p. 130.

14 Imhoff, R., 'Beyond (Right-wing) Authoritarianism: Conspiracy Mentality as an Incremental Predictor of Prejudice', in Bilewicz, M., Cichocka A. and Soral, W. (eds.) *The Psychology of Conspiracy*, London: Routledge, 2015, pp. 122–43; or Van Prooijen, J.-W., Krouwel A. P. W. and Pollet, T. V., 'Political Extremism Predicts Belief in Conspiracy Theories', *Social Psychological and Personality Science* 6(5), 2015: pp. 570–8.

15 Darwin, H., Neave, N. and Holmes, J., 'Belief in Conspiracy Theories: the Role of Paranormal Belief, Paranoid Ideation and Schizotypy', *Personality and Individual Differences* 50, 2011: pp. 1289–93; Swami, V., Pietschnig J., Stieger S. and Voracek, M., 'Alien Psychology: Associations Between Extraterrestrial Beliefs and Paranormal Ideation, Superstitious Beliefs, Schizotypy, and the Big Five Personality Factors', *Applied Cognitive Psychology* 25(4), 2011: pp. 647–53.

16 Thiem, A., 'Conspiracy Theories and Gender and Sexuality', in Butter, M. and Knight, P. (eds.) *The Routledge Handbook of Conspiracy Theories*, London: Routledge, 2019, p. 302. For examples of undercover journalism, see Ginsburg, T., *Die Reise ins Reich: unter Reichsbürgern*, Berlin: Das Neue Berlin, 2018; and, Kay, J., *Among the Truthers: A Journey Through America's Growing Conspiracist Underground*, New York: HarperCollins, 2011.

17 Harambam, J., *Contemporary Conspiracy Culture: Truth and Knowledge in an Era of Epistemic Instability*, London: Routledge, 2020; see also Ward, C. and Voas, D., 'The Emergence of Conspirituality', *Journal of Contemporary Religion* 26(1), 2011: pp. 103–21, doi: 10.1080/13537903.2011.539846.

18 See also Imhoff, R. and Lamberty, P., 'Conspiracy Theories as Psycho-Political Reactions to Perceived Power', in Butter and Knight (eds.) *The Routledge Handbook of Conspiracy Theories*, pp. 192–205.

19 See Bergmann, E. and Butter, M., 'Conspiracy Theory and Populism', in Butter and Knight (eds.) *The Routledge Handbook of Conspiracy Theories*, pp. 330–43.

20 See Oliver, E. J. and Rahn, W. M., 'Rise of the *Trumpenvolk*: Populism in the 2016 Election', *The Annals of the American Academy of Political and Social Science*, 667(1), 2016: pp. 189–206, and Vorländer, H., Herold, M. and Schäller, S.,

PEGIDA: Entwicklung, Zusammensetzung und Deutung einer Empörungsbewegung, Berlin: Springer, 2016, p. 58.

21 Vorländer, Herold and Schäller, *PEGIDA*, p. 58.

22 On Ahmadinejad's conspiracist suspicions, see, for example, Tait, R., 'Mahmoud Ahmadinejad Accuses the West of Destroying Iran's Rain Clouds', *Telegraph*, 10 September 2012, at http://www.telegraph.co.uk/news/worldnews/middleeast/iran/9533842/Mahmoud-Ahmadinejad-accuses-the-West-of-destroying-Irans-rain-clouds.html; and Moore, J., 'Five of Mahmoud Ahmadinejad's Weirdest Conspiracy Theories', *Newsweek*, 12 April 2017, at https://www.newsweek.com/after-throwing-hat-iran-election-five-mahmoud-ahmadinejads-oddest-moments-582837.

23 Kopietz, A., '13-jährige Lisa aus Marzahn: von der Vergewaltigungslüge zum diplomatischen Gewitter', *Berliner Zeitung*, 29 January 2016, at http://www.berliner-zeitung.de/berlin/13-jaehrige-lisa-aus-marzahn-von-der-vergewaltigungsluege-zum-diplomatischen-gewitter-23544190.

24 According to a member of the Task Force, who does not wish to be named, at an event on 25 January 2017 in the EU Parliament in Brussels, where he and I gave lectures on conspiracy theories and fake news.

25 See Avramov, K., Gatov, V. and Yablokov, I., 'Conspiracy Theories and Fake News', in Butter and Knight (eds.) *The Routledge Handbook of Conspiracy Theories*, pp. 512–24.

26 See www.davidicke.com.

27 KenFM, 'KenFM am Telefon: Daniele Ganser über den Anschlag auf Charlie Hebdo – Was wissen wir wirklich?', *YouTube*, 19 January 2015, at https://www.youtube.com/watch?v=CiBWNX-EzRio; Daniele Ganser, 'Dr. Daniele Ganser: Türkei 1980, ein illegaler CIA-Putsch (Köln 3.6.2017)', *YouTube*, 25 February 2019, at https://www.youtube.com/watch?v=XOrngaGwxDQ.

28 Kay, *Among the Truthers*, p. 17.

29 The Alex Jones Channel, 'Alex Jones & Donald Trump Bombshell Full Interview', *YouTube*, 2 December 2015, at https://www.youtube.com/watch?v=FJqLAleEnKw.

30 Ohlheiser, A., '"They Have Broken Trump": Alex Jones and the Trump Internet's Fractured Response to the Syria Strikes', *Washington Post*, 15 April 2018, at https://www.washingtonpost.com/news/the-intersect/wp/2018/04/14/they-have-broken-trump-alex-jones-and-the-trump-internets-furious-response-to-the-syria-strikes/?utm_term=.7b4614febda7; PowerfulJRE, 'Alex Jones Returns!', *YouTube*, 27 February 2019, at https://www.youtube.com/watch?v=-5yh2HcIlkU.

31 HBO, 'Alex Jones: Last Week Tonight with John Oliver', *YouTube*, 30 July 2017, at https://www.youtube.com/watch?v=WyGq6cjcc3Q; Medick, V., 'Der Informationskrieger', *Der Spiegel 9,* 25 February 2017: pp. 90–2; 'InfoWars Publisher Alex Jones Sues PayPal', *BBC News*, 2 October 2018, at https://www.bbc.com/news/technology-45719245.

32 Quoted in Campbell, A., 'Alex Jones Claims "Psychosis" Made Him a Sandy Hook Truther', *Huffpost*, 29 March 2019, at https://www.huffpost.com/entry/alex-jones-blames-conspiracies-on-his-psychosis_n_5c9e1981e4b0bc0daca7202b.

33 Quoted in Killelea, E., 'Alex Jones' Custody Trial: 10 WTF Moments', *Rolling Stone*, 28 April 2017, at https://www.rollingstone.com/culture/culture-news/alex-jones-custody-trial-10-wtf-moments-108404/; quoted in Planas, R., 'Alex Jones Child-Custody Trial Ends With Only a Hint of Conspiracy', *HuffPost*, 27 April 2017, at http://www.huffingtonpost.com/entry/alex-jones-trial-ends_us_59024d96e4b0bb2d086c2f0c; Medick, 'Der Informationskrieger', p. 91.

34 Killelea, 'Alex Jones' Custody Trial: 10 WTF Moments'.

Chapter 4

1 For the idea that conspiracy theories are an anthropological constant, see Groh, D., 'The Temptation of Conspiracy Theory, or: Why Do Bad Things Happen to Good People? Part I: Preliminary Draft of a Theory of Conspiracy Theories', in Graumann, C. F. and Moscovici, S. (eds.) *Changing Conceptions of Conspiracy*, New York: Springer, 1987, pp. 1–13. For a recent psychological study that claims that evolution hard-wired us to believe in conspiracy theories, see Van Prooijen, J.-W. and Van Vugt, M., 'Conspiracy Theories: Evolved Functions and Psychological Mechanisms', *Perspectives on Psychological Science* 13, 2018: pp. 770–88. The relationship between conspiracy theories and rumours is discussed by Astapova, A., 'Rumours, Urban Legends and the Verbal Transmission of Conspiracy Theories', in Butter, M. and Knight, P. (eds.) *The Routledge Handbook of Conspiracy Theories*, London: Routledge, 2020, pp. 391–400.

2 Popper, K., *The High Tide of Prophecy: Hegel, Marx, and the Aftermath*, 4th and rev. edn., Vol. 2 of *The Open Society and Its Enemies*, London: Routledge, 1962 [1945], p. 93, p. 95.

3 Barkun, M., *A Culture of Conspiracy: Apocalyptic Visions in Contemporary America*, 2nd edn., Berkeley: University of California Press, 2013, pp. 41–5. For the relationship between

conspiracy theory and religion, see also the contributions collected in Dyrendal, A., Robertson, D. G. and Asprem, E., *Handbook of Conspiracy Theory and Contemporary Religion*, Leiden: Brill, 2019.

4 Roisman, J., *The Rhetoric of Conspiracy in Ancient Athens*, Berkeley: University of California Press, 2006; Pagán, V. E., *Conspiracy Theory in Latin Literature*, Austin: University of Texas Press, 2012.

5 Roisman, *The Rhetoric of Conspiracy in Ancient Athens*, pp. 72–80, 133–45; Pagán, *Conspiracy Theory in Latin Literature*, pp. 23–7.

6 Tschacher, W., 'Vom Feindbild zur Verschwörungstheorie: Das Hexenstereotyp', in Caumanns, U. and Niendorf, M., *Verschwörungstheorien: Anthropologische Konstanten – Historische Varianten*, Osnabrück: Fibre, 2001, p. 66.

7 Mather, C., *Wonders of the Invisible World*, Boston: no publisher, 1693, p. 86 (italics in original).

8 Zwierlein, C. and De Graaf, B., 'Security and Conspiracy in Modern History', *Security and Conspiracy in History, 16th to 21st Century, special issue of Historical Social Research/ Historische Sozialforschung* 38(1) (143), 2013: pp. 12–15.

9 The articles collected in the volume edited by Coward and Swann provide a good overview of the increasing complexity of conspiracy theories. The volume begins with locally contained witch conspiracies and court intrigues at the beginning of the early modern era and ends with systemic conspiracy theories on the French Revolution; see Coward, B. and Swann, J. (eds.), *Conspiracy Theory in Early Modern Europe: From the Waldensians to the French Revolution*, Aldershot: Ashgate, 2004.

10 Wood, G., 'Conspiracy and the Paranoid Style: Causality and Deceit in the Eighteenth Century', *The William and Mary Quarterly* 39(3), 1982: pp. 413, 416, 417–18, 419. Klausnitzer has shown that the same convictions prevailed in Germany and France at that time; see Klausnitzer, R., *Poesie und Konspiration: Beziehungssinn und Zeichenökonomie von Verschwörungsszenarien in Publizistik, Literatur und Wissenschaft, 1750–1850*, Berlin: de Gruyter, 2007.

11 On the development of this form of public sphere, see Habermas, J., *Strukturwandel der Öffentlichkeit: Untersuchungen zu einer Kategorie der bürgerlichen Gesellschaft* [The Structural Transformation of the Public Sphere], Frankfurt am Main: Suhrkamp, 1990 [1962]; Cubitt, G., 'Conspiracy Myths and Conspiracy Theories', *Journal of the Anthropological Society of Oxford* 20(1), 1989: pp. 12–26.

12 Cubitt, 'Conspiracy Myths and Conspiracy Theories'; Mann, T., *Betrachtungen eines Unpolitischen* [Reflections of a Nonpolitical Man], 2nd edn., Frankfurt am Main: Fischer, 1974 [1918], p. 32 (italics in original).

13 For conspiracy theories in American history, see Butter, M., *Plots, Designs, and Schemes: American Conspiracy Theories from the Puritans to the Present*, Berlin: de Gruyter, 2014.

14 The best study on conspiracy theories about the French Revolution is Oberhauser, C., *Die verschwörungstheoretische Trias: Barruel, Robison, Starck*, Innsbruck: Studien-Verlag, 2013; the accusations against socialists and other groups in nineteenth-century Germany are discussed by Bieberstein, J. R. von, *Die These von der Verschwörung 1776–1945: Philosophen, Freimaurer, Juden, Liberale und Sozialisten als Verschwörer gegen die Sozialordnung*, Frankfurt am Main: Peter Lang, 1976; conspiracy theories about the Jesuits are discussed in Cubitt, G., *The Jesuit Myth: Conspiracy Theory and Politics in Nineteenth-Century France*, Oxford: Clarendon Press, 1993. For an overview of conspiracy theories in Europe in the first half of the twentieth century, see Girard, P., 'Conspiracy Theories in Europe during the Twentieth Century', in Butter and Knight (eds.) *The Routledge Handbook of Conspiracy Theories*, pp. 569–81.

15 See, for example, Knight, P., *Conspiracy Culture: from the Kennedy Assassination to* The X-Files, London: Routledge, 2000.

16 Uscinski, J. E. and Parent, J. M., *American Conspiracy Theories*, Oxford: Oxford University Press, 2014, pp. 110–11; McKenzie-McHarg, A. and Fredheim, R., 'Cock-ups and Slap-downs: a Quantitative Analysis of Conspiracy Rhetoric in the British Parliament 1916–2015', *Historical Methods: A Journal of Quantitative and Interdisciplinary History* 50(3), 2017: pp. 156–69.

17 I owe the distinction between orthodox and heterodox knowledge to Anton, A., *Unwirkliche Wirklichkeiten: zur Wissenssoziologie von Verschwörungstheorien*, Berlin: Logos, 2011.

18 The following explanations are based on the first chapter of Thalmann, K., *The Stigmatization of Conspiracy Theory since the 1950s: 'A Plot to Make Us Look Foolish'*, London: Routledge, 2019.

19 Thalmann, *The Stigmatization of Conspiracy Theory since the 1950s*, p. 35; Lasswell, H. D., *Psychopathology and Politics*, Chicago: University of Chicago Press, 1986 [1930]; Adorno, T. W., Frenkel-Brunswik, E., Levinson, D. J. and Nevitt Sanford,

R., *The Authoritarian Personality*, New York: Harper, 1950; and Löwenthal, L. and Guterman, N., *Prophets of Deceit: a Study of the Techniques of the American Agitator*, New York: Harper, 1949.

20 Popper, *The High Tide of Prophecy*, Vol. 2 of *The Open Society and Its Enemies*, p. 94.

21 Lipset, S. M., 'The Sources of the Radical Right', in Bell, D. (ed.) *The New American Right*, New York: Criterion, 1955, pp. 166–234; Shils, E. A., *The Torment of Secrecy: The Background and Consequences of American Security Politics*, New York: Free Press, 1974 [1956].

22 Bunzel, J. H., *Anti-Politics in America: Reflections on the Anti-Political Temper and Its Distortions of the Democratic Process*, New York: Knopf, 1967; Hofstadter, R., 'The Paranoid Style in American Politics', in *The Paranoid Style in American Politics and Other Essays*, Cambridge, MA: Harvard University Press, 1996 [1964], pp. 3–40.

23 Latour, B., 'Why Has Critique Run out of Steam? From Matters of Fact to Matters of Concern', *Critical Inquiry* 30, 2004: pp. 225–48.

24 See Knight, *Conspiracy Culture*, pp. 117–42. On the connection between conspiracy theory and critical social theory more generally, see Hristov, T., *Impossible Knowledge: Conspiracy Theories, Power, and Truth*, London: Routledge, 2019.

25 Thalmann, *The Stigmatization of Conspiracy Theory since the 1950s*, p. 130; Epstein, E. J., *Inquest: the Warren Commission and the Establishment of Truth*, New York: Viking, 1966; Garrison, J., *On the Trail of the Assassins: My Investigation and Prosecution of the Murder of President Kennedy*, New York: Sheridan Square Press, 1988.

26 Melley, T., *The Covert Sphere: Secrecy, Fiction, and the National Security State*, Ithaca, NY: Cornell University Press, 2013, p. 16.

27 For a more comprehensive treatment of fictional conspiracy scenarios, see Butter, M., 'Conspiracy Theories in Film and Television Shows', in Butter and Knight (eds.) *The Routledge Handbook of Conspiracy Theories*, pp. 457–68.

28 An example of this shortened form of argumentation is Wippermann, W., *Agenten des Bösen: Verschwörungstheorien von Luther bis heute*, Berlin: Be.bra Verlag, 2007, pp. 20–32.

29 Heil, J., *'Gottesfeinde' – 'Menschenfeinde': die Vorstellung von jüdischer Weltverschwörung (13. bis 16. Jahrhundert)*, Essen: Klartext, 2006, pp. 10, 273–4.

30 Heil, *'Gottesfeinde' – 'Menschenfeinde'*, p. 288.

31 Heil, *'Gottesfeinde' – 'Menschenfeinde'*, p. 301.

32 Von Bieberstein, *Die These von der Verschwörung, 1776–1945*, p. 156; on the Jews as profiteers of the revolution, see p. 158; on the Simonini Letter, see p. 161.

33 On authorship, see Hagemeister, M., 'Zur Frühgeschichte der "Protokolle der Weisen von Zion" I: im Reich der Legenden', in Horn, E. and Hagemeister, M. (eds.) *Die Fiktion der jüdischen Weltverschwörung: zu Text und Kontext der 'Protokolle der Weisen von Zion'*, Göttingen: Wallstein, 2012, pp. 140–60; on the lack of anti-Jewish motifs and the presence of the 'Marx-Rothschild Theorem' see Horn, E., 'Das Gespenst der Arkana: Verschwörungsfiktion und Textstruktur der "Protokolle der Weisen von Zion"', in the same volume, pp. 1–25.

34 Horn, 'Das Gespenst der Arkana', pp. 19, 22; Gregory, S., 'Die Fabrik der Fiktionen: Verschwörungsproduktion um 1800', in Horn and Hagemeister (eds.) *Die Fiktion der jüdischen Weltverschwörung*, pp. 51–75.

35 Uptrup, W. M., *Kampf gegen die 'jüdische Weltverschwörung': Propaganda und Antisemitismus der Nationalsozialisten 1919 bis 1945*, Berlin: Metropol, 2003, in particular pp. 91–121; Horn and Hagemeister (eds.) *Die Fiktion der jüdischen Weltverschwörung*, p. xviii.

36 Gedeon, W. [under the pseudonym W. G. Meister], *Christlich-europäische Leitkultur: die Herausforderung Europas durch Säkularismus, Zionismus und Islam*, Frankfurt am Main: R. G. Fischer Verlag, 2009; *Der grüne Kommunismus und die Diktatur der Minderheiten: eine Kritik des westlichen Zeitgeists*, Frankfurt am Main: R. G. Fischer Verlag, 2012; see also Pfahl-Traughber, A., 'Wolfgang Gedeon und die "Protokolle der Weisen von Zion"', *haGalil*, 26 May 2016, at http://www.hagalil.com/2016/05/wolfgang-gedeon.

37 De Poli, B., 'The Judeo-Masonic Conspiracy: the Path from the Cemetery of Prague to Arab Anti-Zionist Propaganda', in Butter, M. and Reinkowski, M. (eds.) *Conspiracy Theories in the United States and the Middle East: A Comparative Approach*, Berlin: de Gruyter, 2014, pp. 251–71; Matussek, C., *Der Glaube an die 'jüdische Weltverschwörung': Die Rezeption der 'Protokolle der Weisen von Zion' in der arabischen Welt*, Münster: LIT Verlag, 2012, p. 25.

38 See Matussek, *Der Glaube an die 'jüdische Weltverschwörung'*, pp. 64–77.

39 ABC News, 'Donald Trump Full Speech at Florida Rally', *YouTube*, 13 October 2016, at https://www.youtube.com/watch?v=Wuy1M05DM38; Herman, E., 'Flüchtlingschaos: Ein merkwürdiger Plan', *Compact*, 31 August 2015, at https://

www.compact-online.de/fluechtlings-chaos-ein-merkwuerdiger-plan; on the image of the octopus, see Baldauf, J. and Rathje, J., 'Neue Weltordnung und "jüdische Weltverschwörung": Antisemitismus und Verschwörungsideologien', in Amadeu Antonio Stiftung (ed.) *'No World Order': wie antisemitische Verschwörungstheorien die Welt verklären*, Berlin, 2015, pp. 45–51, at https://www.amadeu-antonio-stiftung.de/w/files/pdfs/verschwoerungen-internet.pdf.

40 Müller, J.-W., *What Is Populism?*, Philadelphia: University of Pennsylvania Press, 2016, p. 32; Byford, J., *Conspiracy Theories: A Critical Introduction*, Basingstoke: Palgrave Macmillan, 2011, p. 9; Hawkins, K. A. and Rovira Kaltwasser, C., 'What the (Ideational) Study of Populism Can Teach Us, and What It Can't', *Swiss Political Science Review* 23(4), 2017: p. 530. For a more extensive treatment of the theorization provided in this section, see Bergmann, E. and Butter, M., 'Conspiracy Theory and Populism', in Butter and Knight (eds.) *The Routledge Handbook of Conspiracy Theories*, pp. 330–43.

41 Laclau, E., *On Populist Reason*, London: Verso, 2005; Müller, *What Is Populism?*, p. 103.

42 I follow Mudde, C. and Rovira Kaltwasser, C., *Populism: A Very Short Introduction*, Oxford: Oxford University Press, 2017, pp. 5–8.

43 Müller, *What Is Populism?*, p. 22.

44 See also Oliver, E. J. and Rahn, W. M., 'Rise of the *Trumpenvolk*: Populism in the 2016 Election', *The Annals of the American Academy of Political and Social Science* 667(1), 2016: pp. 189–206; and Castanho Silva, B., Vegetti, F. and Littvay, L., 'The Elite is Up to Something: Exploring the Relation Between Populism and Belief in Conspiracy Theories', *Swiss Political Science Review* 23(4), 2017: pp. 423–43.

45 On the conspiracist rhetoric of Hugo Chávez, see Hopper, R., 'Populism and Conspiracy Theory in Latin America: A Case Study of Venezuela', in Butter and Knight (eds.) *The Routledge Handbook of Conspiracy Theories*, pp. 660–73.

46 Fenster, M., *Conspiracy Theories: Secrecy and Power in American Culture*, 2nd edn., Minneapolis: University of Minnesota Press, 2008, p. 84.

47 Hauwaert, S. van, 'Shared Dualisms: On Populism and Conspiracy Theory', *Counterpoint*, at counterpoint.uk.com/shared-dualisms-on-populism-and-conspiracy-theory.

48 For an example of conspiracy theories about the EU and Brexit, see Baxter, D., 'George Soros Plans New World Order EU Superstate Coup', at https://newspunch.com/

182   Notes to pages 118–124

george-soros-plans-new-world-order-eu-superstate-coup;
Weiland, S., '74 Seiten Ausgrenzung: AfD-Parteiprogramm',
Spiegel online, 30 April 2016, at http://www.spiegel.de/
politik/deutschland/afd-programm-so-sieht-die-partei-die-welt-
a-1089976.html.

49 According to the sociologist Thomas Lengsfeld writing about
the voters of AfD in Bidder, B., 'Der Gerechtigkeitswahlkampf
der SPD war nicht klug', *Spiegel online*, 23 September 2017, at
http://www.spiegel.de/wirtschaft/soziales/afd-im-aufwind-der-
gerechtigkeitswahlkampf-der-spd-war-nicht-klug-a-1169313.
html (italics in original).

50 Ehrenfreund, M., 'The Outlandish Conspiracy Theories Many
of Donald Trump's Supporters Believe', *Washington Post*, 5
May 2016, at https://www.washingtonpost.com/news/wonk/
wp/2016/05/05/the-outlandish-conspiracy-theories-many-of-
donald-trumps-supporters-believe/?utm_term=.3696856b0efc;
for the first results of this study, see Hammel, L. L.,
'Verschwörungsglaube, Populismus und Protest', *Politikum* 3,
2017: pp. 32–41.

51 See Ylä-Anttila, T., 'Populist Knowledge: "Post-truth"
Repertoires of Contesting Epistemic Authorities', *European
Journal of Cultural and Political Sociology* 5(4), 2017, at https://
doi.org/10.1080/23254823.2017.1414620.

Chapter 5

1 For example Peter Boehringer, who entered the Bundestag via
the Bavarian state list of the AfD; for a comparison of him and
others see Leber, S., 'So extrem sind die Kandidaten der AfD', *Der
Tagesspiegel*, 21 September 2017, at http://www.tagesspiegel.
de/themen/reportage/rechte-vor-einzug-in-den-bundestag-
so-extrem-sind-die-kandidaten-der-afd/20350578.html.

2 Freyermuth, G. S., 'Sie beobachten uns: Verschwörungstheorien
blühen erst im Internet richtig auf', *c't: Magazin für
Computertechnik*, 18 June 1998, at https://www.heise.de/ct/
artikel/Sie-beobachten-uns-286410.html; see also Schetsche, M.,
'Die ergoogelte Wirklichkeit: Verschwörungstheorien und das
Internet', *Telepolis*, 4 May 2005, at https://www.heise.de/tp/
features/Die-ergoogelte-Wirklichkeit-3439523.html.

3 Weisberg, H., *Whitewash: The Report on the Warren Report*,
no location given: Weisberg, 1965. For the best overview on
the diversity of conspiracy theories on the Kennedy assassination, see Knight, P., *The Kennedy Assassination*, Edinburgh:
Edinburgh University Press, 2007, pp. 75–104.

4 For a detailed analysis of the aesthetics of the *Loose Change* films, see Butter, M. and Retterath, L., 'From Alerting the World to Affirming Its Own Community: The Shifting of Cultural Work of the *Loose Change* Films', *Canadian Review of American Studies* 40(1), 2010: pp. 25–44.

5 Sales, N. J., 'Click Here for Conspiracy', *Vanity Fair*, 10 October 2006, at https://www.vanityfair.com/news/2006/08/loosechange200608. The original version of *Loose Change* is no longer available on YouTube. The later versions are easy to find with the search function.

6 The argument for the steady increase is made, for example, by Olmsted, K. S., *Real Enemies: Conspiracy Theories and American Democracy, World War I to 9/11*, Oxford: Oxford University Press, 2009, pp. 145–8. The more convincing counterargument is made by Thalmann, K., *The Stigmatization of Conspiracy Theory since the 1950s: 'A Plot to Make us Look Foolish'*, London: Routledge, 2019, p. 112.

7 Thalmann, *The Stigmatization of Conspiracy Theory*, p. 112.

8 911-Archiv.net, at http://www.911-archiv.net; Ivry, D., 'LBJ Knew Who Killed JFK' (2018), at https://blogs.timesofisrael.com/lbj-knew-who-killed-jfk; Webb, W., 'Washington Follows Ukraine, Syria Roadmap in Push for Venezuela Regime Change' (2019), at https://www.mintpressnews.com/us-follows-ukraine-syria-roadmap-in-venezuela-regime-change-push/254265.

9 Birchall, C., *Knowledge Goes Pop: From Conspiracy Theory to Gossip*, Oxford: Berg, 2006, offers an excellent discussion of the broader development towards a dehierarchization of different forms of knowledge, of which what is happening online is only a part.

10 Uscinski, J. E., DeWitt, D. and Atkinson, M. D., 'A Web of Conspiracy? Internet and Conspiracy Theory', in Dyrendal, A., Robertson, D. G. and Asprem, E. *Handbook of Conspiracy Theory and Contemporary Religion*, Leiden: Brill, 2019, pp. 106–29.

11 Oliver, E. and Wood, T., 'Conspiracy Theories and the Paranoid Style(s) of Mass Opinion', *American Journal of Political Science* 58(4), 2014: pp. 952–66.

12 Del Vicario, M. et al., 'The Spreading of Misinformation Online', *PNAS* 113(3), 2016: pp. 554–9.

13 'Trump Adviser's Son Loses Transition Team Job for Spreading Fake News', *Guardian*, 7 December 2016, at https://www.theguardian.com/us-news/2016/dec/07/trump-adviser-son-michael-flynn-sacked-pizzagate-comet-ping-pong-restaurant; 'Umstrittener AfD-Politiker Gedeon verlässt Fraktion', *Welt*,

5 July 2016, at https://www.welt.de/politik/deutschland/
article156842643/Umstrittener-AfD-Politiker-Gedeon-
verlaesst-Fraktion.html; Pearson, A., 'It's Beginning to Look
a Lot Like a Brexit Conspiracy', *Telegraph*, 20 November
2018, at https://www.telegraph.co.uk/politics/2018/11/20/
beginning-look-lot-like-brexit-conspiracy.

14 See Lütjen, T., *Die Politik der Echokammer: Wisconsin und die
ideologische Polarisierung der USA*, Bielefeld: Transcript, 2016,
pp. 21–60.

15 On the fragmentation of the media landscape, see Thalmann,
The Stigmatization of Conspiracy Theory since the 1950s, pp.
293–5.

16 According to Uscinski, J. and Parent, J., *American Conspiracy
Theories*, New York: Oxford University Press, 2014, pp. 125–6,
138–44, it is not so much political polarization as such that
drives conspiracy theories about Republicans among Democrats
and vice versa, but the experience of defeat in election. When
Democrats are in power, they argue, conspiracy theories thrive
among Republicans; when Republicans are governing, it is the
other way around.

17 Brunner, K. and Ebitsch, S., 'In der rechten Echokammer',
Süddeutsche Zeitung, 1 May 2017, at http://www.sueddeutsche.de/
politik/politik-im-netz-in-der-rechten-echokammer-1.3485685.

18 Pennekamp, J. and Bernau, P., 'Die Angstindustrie',
Frankfurter Allgemeine Zeitung, 17 May 2015, at http://
www.faz.net/aktuell/wirtschaft/unternehmen/verlage-und-
unternehmen-rund-um-verschwoerungstheorien-13374395.
html?printPagedArticle=true#pageIndex_2; cf. Kopp Verlag;
and Hunger, A., 'Gut vernetzt – Der Kopp-Verlag und die schil-
lernde rechte Publizistenszene', in Braun, S., Geisler, A., and
Gerster, M. *Strategien der extremen Rechten*, 2nd edn., Berlin:
Springer, 2016, pp. 425–40.

19 This is based on a statement from 18 September 2017 by
the director of the library of contemporary history, Christian
Westerhoff, during a lecture I gave there.

20 See Schultz, T., Jackob, N., Ziegele, M. Quiring, O. and Schemer,
C., 'Erosion des Vertrauens zwischen Medien und Publikum?',
Media Perspektiven 5, 2017: pp. 246–59; and Zick, A., Küpper,
B. and Berghan, W., *Verlorene Mitte – Feindselige Zustände:
Rechtsextreme Einstellungen in Deutschland 2018/19*, Bonn:
Dietz, 2019.

21 Weiland, S., '74 Seiten Ausgrenzung: AfD-Parteiprogramm',
Spiegel online, 30 April 2016, at http://www.spiegel.de/
politik/deutschland/afd-programm-so-sieht-die-partei-die-welt-

a-1089976.html; on the email affair, see 'AfD-Spitzenkandidatin Weidel plötzlich kleinlaut', *Frankfurter Allgemeine Zeitung*, 17 September 2017, at http://www.faz.net/aktuell/politik/alice-weidel-spricht-offenbar-nicht-mehr-von-faelschung-15202774.html.

22 Quote taken from Ruta-Franke, G., 'Palin Flirts With Obama Birth Certificate Questions', *Washington Post*, 4 December 2009, at http://voices.washingtonpost.com/44/2009/12/palin-flirts-with-obama-birth.html; and Amira, D., 'Kansas Congressional Candidate *Just Can't* Stop Accidentally Being a Birther', *Nymag.com*, 23 July 2010, at http://nymag.com/daily/intelligencer/2010/07/kansas_congressional_candidate.html.

23 Fenster, M., *Conspiracy Theories: Secrecy and Power in American Culture*, 2nd edn., Minneapolis: University of Minnesota Press, 2008, pp. 182–94.

24 Cf. Fenster, *Conspiracy Theories*, pp. 162–3.

25 NullClothing, 'Zeitgeist – The Movie: Federal Reserve', *YouTube*, 16 June 2007, at https://www.youtube.com/watch?v=_dmPchuXIXQ.

26 Schickentanz, B., 'NOTRE-DAME in Flammen, Unfall oder 'REICHSTAGSBRAND' (2019), at https://www.facebook.com/550805391725433/videos/notre-dame-in-flammen-unfall-oder-reichstagsbrand/383598742493224.

27 Although it can be argued that the final cut version of *Loose Change* is itself primarily aimed at viewers who are already convinced of the conspiracy; cf. Butter, M. and Retterath, L., 'From Alerting the World to Stabilizing Its Own Community: the Shifting Cultural Work of the *Loose Change* Films', *Canadian Review of American Studies* 40, 2010: pp. 25–44.

28 Due to public pressure, YouTube deleted some of these videos, but some of them were quickly uploaded again under different titles. For an example relating to the Las Vegas assassination, see https://www.youtube.com/watch?v=ZhGhLPGQhlQ.

29 Agent S, 'Body Double – PROOF!', *YouTube*, 14 September 2016, at https://www.youtube.com/watch?v=1w3NFTzyMmg.

30 The tweets on this topic that Trump himself later deleted are at http://www.trumptwitterarchive.com/highlights/birtherism. On Trump's strategic use of the allegations, see Parker, A. and Eder, S., 'Inside the Six Weeks Donald Trump Was a Nonstop "Birther"!', *New York Times*, 2 July 2016, at https://www.nytimes.com/2016/07/03/us/politics/donald-trump-birther-obama.html.

31 For this and other examples, see DelReal, J. A., 'Here Are 10 More Conspiracy Theories Embraced By Donald Trump',

Washington Post, 16 September 2016, at https://www. washingtonpost.com/news/post-politics/wp/2016/09/16/ here-are-10-more-conspiracy-theories-embraced-by-donald-trump/?utm_term=.7c0fae64d1be.

32 Newsy, 'Donald Trump Tries To Connect Ted Cruz's Father To JFK Assassination', *YouTube*, 3 May 2016, at https://www. youtube.com/watch?v=u1ND2VS8q08.

33 ABC News, 'Donald Trump Full Speech at Florida Rally', *YouTube*, 13 October 2016, at https://www.youtube.com/ watch?v=Wuy1M05DM38.

34 See Rothwell, J. T., 'Explaining Nationalist Political Views: The Case of Donald Trump', *SSRN*, 2 November 2016, at https:// papers.ssrn.com/sol3/papers.cfm?abstract_id=2822059.

35 Thalmann, *The Stigmatization of Conspiracy Theory*, p. 192.

Conclusion

1 'Armed Protesters Demonstrate against Covid-19 Lockdown at Michigan Capitol', *Guardian*, 30 April 2020, at https:// www.theguardian.com/us-news/2020/apr/30/michigan-protests-coronavirus-lockdown-armed-capitol.

2 Polehanki, D., Twitter, 30 April 2020, at https://twitter.com/ SenPolehanki/status/1255899318210314241; Trump, D., 'LIBERATE MICHIGAN!', Twitter, 17 April 2020, at https:// twitter.com/realdonaldtrump/status/1251169217531056130.

3 See Fenster, M., *Conspiracy Theories: Secrecy and Power in American Culture*, 2nd edn., Minneapolis: University of Minnesota Press, 2008, pp. 52–90.

4 Cobain, I., Parveen, N. and Taylor, M., 'The Slow-Burning Hatred that Led Thomas Mair to Murder Jo Cox', *Guardian*, 23 November 2016, at https://www.theguardian.com/uk-news/2016/ nov/23/thomas-mair-slow-burning-hatred-led-to-jo-cox-murder.

5 Bartlett, J. and Miller, C., *The Power of Unreason: Conspiracy Theories, Extremism and Counter-Terrorism*, London: Demos, 2010, pp. 4–5, at https://www.demos.co.uk/files/Conspiracy_ theories_paper.pdf?1282913891; Lee, B. 'Radicalisation and Conspiracy Theories', in Butter and Knight (eds.), *Routledge Handbook of Conspiracy Theories*, p. 354.

6 Jolley, D. and Douglas, K., 'The Social Consequences of Conspiracism: Exposure to Conspiracy Theories Decreases Intentions to Engage in Politics and to Reduce One's Carbon Footprint', *British Journal of Psychology* 105(1), 2014: pp. 35–56; Müller, *What Is Populism?*, pp. 31–2.

7 Wikipedia, 'Crisis Actor', https://en.wikipedia.org/wiki/

Crisis_actor; Hagen, D., 'Xavier Naidoo: Nach Tod von George Floyd – Sänger stellt irre Theorie auf', *Mannheim 24*, 8 June 2020, at https://www.mannheim24.de/mannheim/xavier-naidoo-george-floyd-tot-theorie-usa-demos-rassismus-saenger-telegram-mannheim-video-13786017.html.

8 Bartlett and Miller, *The Power of Unreason*, p. 4; Lee, 'Radicalisation', p. 354.

9 Nyhan, B. and Reifler, J., 'Does Correcting Myths About the Flu Vaccine Work? An Experimental Evaluation of the Effects of Corrective Information', *Vaccine* 33(3), 2015: pp. 459–64; Zollo, F., Bessi, A., Del Vicario, M., Scala, A., Caldarelli,G., Shekhtman, L., Havlin, S. and Quattrociocchi, W., 'Debunking in a World of Tribes', *PLOS ONE*, 2017, 12.

10 Cook, J. and Lewandowsky, S., *The Debunking Handbook*, St. Lucia: University of Queensland, 2011, pp. 39–42, at https://www.skepticalscience.com/docs/Debunking_Handbook.pdf; see also Rathje, J., Kahane, A., Baldauf, J. and Lauer, S., *'No World Order': Wie antisemitische Verschwörungstheorien die Welt verklären*, Berlin: Amadeu Antonio Stiftung, 2015, at https://www.amadeu-antonio-stiftung.de/w/files/pdfs/verschwoerungen-internet.pdf.

11 Jolley, D. and Douglas, K. M., 'Prevention is Better than Cure: Addressing Anti-Vaccine Conspiracy Theories', *Journal of Applied Social Psychology* 47, 2017: pp. 459–69.

Index